BROWN GIRLS

DAPHNE
PALASI ANDREADES

4th ESTATE • *London*

4th Estate
An imprint of HarperCollins*Publishers*
1 London Bridge Street
London SE1 9GF

www.4thEstate.co.uk

HarperCollins*Publishers*
1st Floor, Watermarque Building, Ringsend Road
Dublin 4, Ireland

First published in Great Britain in 2022 by 4th Estate
First published in the United States in 2022 by Random House

1

Book design by Jo Anne Metsch

A catalogue record for this book is
available from the British Library

ISBN 978-0-00-847805-6 (hardback)
ISBN 978-0-00-847806-3 (trade paperback)

Set in Walbaum MT Std
Printed and bound in the UK using 100%
renewable electricity at CPI Group (UK) Ltd

MIX
Paper from
responsible sources
FSC™ C007454

This book is produced from independently certified FSC™ paper
to ensure responsible forest management.

For more information visit: www.harpercollins.co.uk/green

Praise for *Brown Girls*:

'A masterful triumph by a brilliant new author with an original voice. It's an unforgettable novel written with pride, love, and tears. Andreades's spare yet richly detailed writing makes the heart ache for every brown girl whose desire is to be seen and, most of all, heard.'

NICOLE DENNIS-BENN,
bestselling author of *Patsy*

'A glorious anthem of a book, written effortlessly, ingeniously, in a vibrant choral voice. It sings, it aches, it shimmers; it leaps from the page with pure life. I loved it.'   LUCY CALDWELL, author of *Intimacies*

'I just swallowed this book and was swallowed by it in return. For those of us who were once teenage girls, it is an irresistible chorus of remembrances. For those of us who are New Yorkers, it is also an ode to Queens, and the multi-ethnic first-person plural sounds like the borough itself, rich and varied and glorious. I absolutely loved this book.'

EMMA STRAUB, author of *All Adults Here*

'A beautiful story of sisterhood between a group of girls from Queens, how they navigate life from girlhood to adulthood and the different paths they take. It's no exaggeration to say this novel completely absorbed me. Daphne is a masterful storyteller, and this is an absolutely breath-taking debut.'

SARA JAFARI, author of *The Mismatch*

'A poetic story for anyone who has longed to leave home, only to find that home resides within you.'

SANDRA CISNEROS, author of
The House on Mango Street

For brown girls everywhere

&

for Thad

Give me your tired, your poor,

Your huddled masses yearning to breathe free

—EMMA LAZARUS, "The New Colossus"

PART ONE

BROWN GIRLS

WE LIVE IN THE DREGS OF QUEENS, NEW YORK, WHERE airplanes fly so low that we are certain they will crush us. On our block, a lonely tree grows. Its branches tangle in power lines. Its roots upend sidewalks where we ride our bikes before they are stolen. Roots that render the concrete slabs uneven, like a row of crooked teeth. In front yards, not to be confused with actual lawns, grandmothers string laundry lines, hang bedsheets, our brothers' shorts, and our sneakers scrubbed to look brand-new. *Take those down!* our mothers hiss. *This isn't back home.* In front yards grow tomatoes that have fought their way through the hard earth.

Our grandmothers refuse canes. Our brothers dress in wifebeaters. We all sit on stoops made of brick. The Italian boys with their shaved heads zoom by on bikes, staring, their laughter harsh as their shiny gold chains.

Our grandparents weed their gardens and our brothers smoke their cigarettes and, in time, stronger substances we cannot recognize. Whose scent makes our heads pulse. Our brothers, who ride on bikes, lifting their front wheels high into the air.

"BROWN"

I F YOU REALLY WANT TO KNOW, WE ARE THE COLOR OF 7-Eleven root beer. The color of sand at Rockaway Beach when it blisters the bottoms of our feet. Color of soil. Color of the charcoal pencils our sisters use to rim their eyes. Color of grilled hamburger patties. Color of our mother's darkest thread, which she loops through the needle. Color of peanut butter. Of the odd gene that makes us *fair and white as snow,* like whatsername, is it Snow White? But don't get it twisted—we're still brown. Dark as 7 P.M. dusk, when our mothers switch on lights in empty rooms. Exclaim, *Oh! There you are.*

THE DREGS OF QUEENS

THE SIGHTS IN OUR HOMETOWN: CENTRAL ROAD NICK-named the "Boulevard of Death" by the *New York Post*, which snakes through our neighborhood like a long gray tongue. Mimi's Salon with an ad that reads, MANI N PEDI, $15.99! W/ NECK MASSAGE FREE. Down the boulevard, across the street from the auto repair shop: a branch of the New York Public Library. Book pages smeared with fingerprints, a booger, the remnant of a sneeze. In the corner, a homeless man fortressed by plastic bags snoozes peacefully. We know he's different from the guy who raps his knuckles on car windows and asks, *Little girl, got any change?* before our parents zoom away. Welcome to the dregs of Queens: White Castle sign that comes into view when our subway pulls into the station, tracks rumbling above a Honda minivan, a halal food cart called RAFI SMILES with the

scent of bubbling oil and smoke that wafts past a forgotten discount electronics store now selling mattresses.
Train slogs above a man chomping a Boston cream donut,
whose custard filling explodes onto the tips of his fingers. He licks them, waits for the Q11 to arrive. Ray's
Not Your Mama's Pizzeria with spongy Sicilian slices
whose Cheetos-colored oil trickles down our chins when
we take a bite. Soap 'n Suds Laundromat filled with
steel machines pounding round and round. A Chinese-
Mexican takeout joint beside O'Malley's, whose carpet
of plastic green grass out front is littered with cigarette
butts. Our own houses: neat brick rectangles. Hidden,
peripheral. Sometimes the sun shines here.

DUTIES

BUT WE BROWN GIRLS ARE TEN AND ALREADY KNOW HOW to be good. How to cross the Boulevard of Death, hand in hand with younger siblings to reach public school courtyards, how to trick and bribe and coax them to finish their homework (*In 1492*, they recite, *Columbus sailed the ocean blue*). How to mouth SHHH! when our fathers have fallen asleep on couches after long shifts, and how to vacuum homes, carpets dotted with hair and cookie crumbs. We know how to muscle these bagpipes up and down dim staircases, even though they are heavier than us. We know never to talk back. We know how to cram into our parents' beds when loved ones from distant lands and warm climates immigrate to the States with their suitcases and dreams and empty wallets. Stay for months, years.

One aunt gives us manicures every Sunday. Another squirts poop-colored henna onto our palms, sketches lotus flowers. One cousin lets us listen to her collection of country CDs—Dolly, Shania, Faith Hill—her most prized possessions. *Wide open spaces!* we sing along with the Dixie Chicks. Another cousin lends us her romance novel, the lone paperback that sits atop her dresser, after we beg her. We'd glimpsed its cover of a woman clinging to a man's bare, muscled chest. The image excites us. We re-create it by standing in front of fans to mimic that hair-blowing-in-the-wind effect. We top it off with our best lovesick expressions. Until we grow bored of pretending to be these women. We sprinkle salt onto slugs instead.

Our parents take us aside one night. *If anyone asks, we're the only ones who live here, okay?*

Though we don't fully understand, we know how to keep our families' secrets.

When our cousins and aunts and uncles leave for new jobs in new cities—they are nannies and construction workers, cooks and caretakers—we feel a sinking sorrow. It doesn't matter if we don't share a drop of blood with these people; we have been taught to call them family. When they depart, we do not cry. We do not cling on. We are good girls. Instead, we prepare for going-away parties, which last all through the night and end with us falling asleep on couches, waking the next day in beds we share with our younger siblings. We wake to the scent of garlic and bonfire smoke still lingering in our hair, traces of cake and drool crusted on our cheeks. No matter.

Before these parties begin, however, we must get ready. We have exactly seven minutes in bathrooms. We remember to wash our hair with cold water—*Hurry up, I need to go!*—so that it grows thick and shiny.

BRAS

I N KITCHENS REDOLENT WITH GARLIC AND ONIONS, BROWN girls stand, hovering over pans, cracking open brown eggs, stirring them just so and frying them. We lie, starfish-like and still, atop sun-warmed concrete in backyards. We sing Mariah, Whitney, Destiny's Child, our voices straining for the same notes as these brown singers. *Say my name, say my name*, we harmonize with Beyoncé, Kelly, Michelle. In bedrooms, we adjust training bras for the first time. *Hook it like this under your rib cage. Now twist it back around.* Some of us are experts on bras because we've observed our mothers with their sagging breasts and *areolas*, a word we learned, eyes glued to our sisters' discarded puberty books (*Celebrate Your Body!*). When we view our mothers' breasts for the first time, we are filled with repulsion and fascination. We wrap our arms around our own flat chests to hide them. *After you've had four kids,* our mothers explain, *they get this way. You'll see.* Some of us are experts because we've observed our sisters. *This one's a T-shirt bra. This one's a push-up. This one's got straps that crisscross at your back. This one has lace and you should only wear it to parties.* Why? we ask. *Because anywhere else, people will just think you're a slut—trust me.* We are experts because we've peeped through cracks right before our sisters shut their bedroom doors, boyfriends trailing behind them. Our parents are away working their usual twelve-, fourteen-hour shifts. *Shhh!* our sisters whispered to us, fingers to their lips.

Brown girls singing, jumping, spinning. Brown girls screeching Mariah at the top of their lungs, cackling in the school courtyard, playing handball, talking smack.

LUNCHROOM

WHY DON'T YOU SHUT THE FUCK UP, JOSEPH JUSTIN O'Brien says to our friend Trish, *and go back to the projects you came from?* We deliberate whether or not to take matters into our own hands and beat the shit out of Joseph Justin O'Brien because would the lunch ladies *really* understand if we told them what he said? Would they even care? So, in the end, we decide against carrying out our scheme because A) Everyone already knows Joseph Justin O'Brien and all his friends are racist, that they *definitely* would've been a part of the KKK (But seriously—does the KKK still exist?), and B) We're terrified of what our parents would do if we got in trouble at school. We imagine our punishments: rubber slippers to asses, brooms to asses, belts to asses, hands coiling swiftly around our arms followed by a merciless beating of our asses—and already, our backsides ache. Though that asshole, that *sphincter* (another word we've stolen from our older sisters' biology text-books) really *does* deserve it, we tell Trish, who does not even live in the projects. Instead, we eat our chicken patty sandwiches, baked at 350 degrees in industrial ovens, and topped with squirts of ketchup. Lunches provided by New York City via the U.S. government, the same meals that prison inmates eat—that's what our Social Studies teacher Mr. DiMarco told us. We promise Trish that we will take our revenge another time. But not before we pluck the limp broccoli from our trays and fling the pieces at Joseph Justin's fat head. Bullseye! When we hear the satisfying squelch followed by Joseph Justin's bellow of outrage, we high-five each other. We wrap our arms around Trish and cheer.

Brown girls, age eleven. Who drink white milk and sit at the white lunch table. Brown girls being brown.

MUSICAL CHAIRS

OUR TEACHERS CALL ON NADIRA BUT STARE AT ANJALI. Our teachers tell Michaela to *Come to the board and answer number three and make sure you show your work, please,* even though they hand the whiteboard marker to Naz. We stand when our names are called, and our teachers halt, confused. *Oh, I'm sorry, I— No, not you, I didn't mean you, I—* Across the classroom, we catch each other's gazes. Nadira is Pakistani and wears a headscarf, which drapes elegantly beneath her neck, except for when she's playing handball and she knots the fabric, tight, under her chin. Anjali is Guyanese, and her braid looks like a thick rope that lays heavy against her back, curly baby hairs tamed by coconut oil. Michaela is Haitian and likes to mimic her parents' French accents on the school bus (Take zee twash out! she says, as we clutch our sides in laughter), and Naz's family is from the Ivory Coast—I mean, we're practically cousins, she says to Michaela. Our teachers snap at Sophie to *STOP TALKING NOW,* but call her Mae's name. Sophie, who is Filipino, clamps a hand over her big-ass mouth, which is never closed—she loves to gossip and flirt with the boys we call "Spanish"—while Mae, who is Chinese and polite to teachers, at least to their faces, jolts from the bookshelf where she's stealthily shuffling novels from their alphabetical spots, in order to disrupt our English class two periods later. We laugh at our teachers, though our eyes tighten. Our classmates roar with glee at their errors and purposely call us the wrong names for the rest of the week, too. They call us Khadija, Akanksha, Maribeth, Ximena, Breonna, Cherelle, Thanh, Yoon, Ellen. They call us Josie, Rukhsana, Sonia, Odalis, Annabel, Kyra, Jenny, Cindy, Esther. During lunchtime, we call our teachers different names, too: dumbass, idiot, old-lady bitch. We steal a permanent marker, scrawl STOOPID on their classroom doors, above posters that read *Knowledge. Wisdom. Discipline.* From the corner of our eyes, we study each other while we hold our Styrofoam lunch trays, wait on bus stops, and stretch in gym class, our sneakers skidding against scuffed floors. Think: Her body is not mine is not mine is not mine. And yet.

DO NOW: WHAT DO YOU WANT TO BE WHEN YOU GROW UP?

FOR TODAY'S WRITING WARM-UP, WE JOT DOWN OUR responses in marble notebooks:

- My mom's boss, the banker who works for Morgan Stanley, whose house she cleans twice a week (She snuck me in yesterday.)
- Vanessa Kleinberg, who brushes her hair during the Pledge of Allegiance. Twenty times on the right side of her head and twenty times on the left, as we and the rest of the class watch, rapt.
- Rihanna—her dance moves are cool as fuck, plus, she has the same skin tone as me.
- A pediatrician (MY mom says I can be anything. Actually, a doctor is all she wants me to be.) (Ana, SHUT UP, you're gonna get us in trouble!)

- Miss America (Oh. My. Gosh. Zainab, are you for real? Mrs. Lester's going to *kill* you.)
- Miss Universe (The past two were Filipino. My uncles say this is proof we're the most B-E-A-UTIFUL women in the world!) (Ccchhh, as if, Rosaria!)
- Fuck Miss America AND Miss Universe! I don't want to be some stupid-ass beauty queen. I want to make some serious $$$CASH MONEY$$$. You know—*Bill Gates* type of money. Cha-ching! (Yeah, but you ain't half as smart, Natalie.)
- I want to do whatever my older brother's doing. He got mad pissed at me the other day for stealing his hoodie—from behind, my mom thought I was him.
- I want to be an artist. (But my dad says art's just a hobby. He told me to do something practical. Be an accountant like my cousin, Bernice. So I guess I'll be an accountant.)
- Accountant

BROWN BOYS

WE STARE AT BROWN BOYS WITH THEIR OBSIDIAN HAIR, their cheekbones, and think: He looks like my brother. He looks like the boy from the restaurant where we ordered kabobs, lechón, jerk chicken, plátanos. He looks like the boy at the bodega who rang up our barbecue chips, our ninety-nine-cent cans of iced tea. He's beautiful, we think, but we'd never go *out* with him. We'd never *date* him. Why? Because he doesn't look— you know. Because he looks like— And anyway, he only likes *those* kinds of girls, the Vanessa Kleinberg types, we heard him say so. We stare at brown boys, listen to the way they say *lie-berry*. They fascinate us, but we ignore them. Except for one day when our class goes down for a visit to the library—Lie-brair-ree, we mouth, alone with brown boys behind a bookshelf. Library. Follow my lips. Say it like this.

OTHER BOYS

WE SWEAR WE FALL IN L— SHHH, DON'T SAY IT, HE'LL hear you, what are you stupid, or something? Have you lost your freaking mind? Christ! Golden hair, eyes the color of the sky on a cloudless day, and most important, skin as fair as our mothers' whitening creams. We adore them, these boys who, if we squint, resemble posters of the heartthrobs tacked to our bedroom walls, ones we'd torn from our sisters' magazines. Boy-band boys, boys with names like Aaron and Zack and Jake and Brad, boys with faces like in the ads plastered around Queens Center mall, Target, and Kmart, faces that make us halt and shift uncomfortably due to the stickiness that's suddenly present in our underpants. All-American boys. That boy is FI-I-I-I-NE! we say to each other. It's because he's got that *hair* and those *eyes*! Sigh. I could stare at him all *day*. We watch from afar as

these white boys hold hands with the Jessicas and Kate-
lyns and Claires of our grade. While we daydream that
it is us they take on their fathers' boats for midnight
swims. If only we knew how to swim. Brown girls brown
girls brown girls who profess a deep, unshakeable love
for these boys who sometimes see them, but mostly
don't.

GIRLS LIKE YOU

WE TAKE BUSES—THE 53, 22, THE 11—THAT GROAN TO A halt at each stoplight. Meet me at the mall! We are thirteen. We amble through all four floors, but don't buy much. A coral-colored lip gloss, a T-shirt from the clearance rack printed with an eagle and an American flag because Gabby's favorite holiday is the Fourth of July. We splurge on nine-dollar nail polish packaged in graceful, glossy bottles with pigments that leave our nails iridescent. In the food court, we stick our fingers into each other's french fries zigzagged with ketchup, munch on limp slices of quesadilla, and slurp extra-large orange sodas. We walk into a boutique with track lights on the ceiling that make every item—the high heels we cannot balance in, the cubic zirconia necklaces, the beaded sweaters, and tulle dresses—appear glamorous. We press clothing, draped on hangers, to our bodies.

Stylish, confident—maybe we could be these girls. We laugh and hurry to the fitting room. Leila tries on a sea-foam green polo shirt, pops up its stiff collar, and we baptize her Miss Preppy. We zip Aisha into a fuchsia gown, squeal, Oooh, Hollywood glam! and call her Diva. We try on a black dress with a scoop neck and a bow tie above our tailbones, but immediately shrug it off—too serious, too boring.

We are interrupted by a pounding on our dressing room doors. An angry voice claiming to be the manager. *What are you girls doing in there?* The doorknob jangles. *You better not be stealing anything!* she shouts. *I know what girls like you do!* (Girls like us?) *Come out! Right now!* Startled, we fumble to tug our jeans over our legs, which are in need of moisturizer. Our purses hang by mirrors and are ridiculously small. They carry nothing more than quarters for our bus rides home, cellphones passed down from sisters, and one carefully folded twenty-dollar bill—our hard-earned babysitting cash— to "shop." What clothes could possibly fit in here? The manager pounds again. *Open up!* she screams. We hear a key slip into the lock. The door swings open.

Observe brown girls, thirteen-year-old specimens: fine dark hairs sprouting from unshaven and unwaxed arm-pits and bikini lines, jagged stretch marks that resemble lightning bolts on stomachs and hips, arms tangled in T-shirts pulled halfway over their heads. Standing in their white cotton underwear.

FAMILY PARTIES

AT KITCHEN TABLES LINED WITH PLACE MATS COMMEMO-rating a coveted summer vacation to ORLANDO! we serve coffee and tea and extra helpings to aunties and uncles and grandparents while little cousins dart between our legs. Cut the cake, refill the drinks. *My, what a woman you've become!* our aunts say. *Stay thin, not like me. Did you gain weight? Are you eating enough? We don't like your hair*—they frown—*why did you dye it blond? No, it suits you, but go to this hairdresser next time, he's cheaper.* We grow dizzy at their advice, at their, what do you call it? Love.

The party swells and our families grow drunk on wine and memories. *My brother, you remember him, the troublemaker? Well, when he was seventeen, he brought home this girl while our parents were in the fields. Three months later, the girl—she must've been fifteen—was*

pregnant, and they were on their way to being married!
Another story: *I hated harvest season. My shoulders
ached from leaning over to pick these tiny grains of rice.
At the end of the day, I cried and cried and told my
grandmother, I never want to do this AGAIN! And as
soon as I was old enough, I left the provinces for the capital. I buried my grandmother the next year.*

We slip from houses that feel too warm and suffocating. Outside, we exhale. We sit on bike handlebars and
sidewalk edges as the sun sets a drunken orange. On the
radio, Mariah sings, *Gimme your love*, repeats this line
ten, fifteen times. "Heartbreaker." Because we do not
want to go back inside, we wander past the gas station,
the park, observe the houses that grow grander, with fat
trees casting lengthy shadows. Where no laundry lines
are strung. These houses, with their perfect symmetry
and silence, frighten us. We're reminded of our families' laughter and shouts in crowded kitchens and backyards. The earth grows darker. We run home—past God
Bless Deli 2, past the beat-up Mustang with the man
tinkering underneath, past the Italian boys on their
stoops. Who call out, *Ay, beauduhful!* when we zoom by.

Beautiful? we think, startled. When did we become
beautiful?

OPTICAL ILLUSIONS

GIVE IT TO ME—GIVE IT TO ME! NOT LIKE THAT, IDIOT! Like this. There. We draw on perfect eyebrows, arched and full, but not too dark like Auntie Luccia's, whose tatted brows resemble inky, stern tadpoles. We borrow our sisters' tubes of concealer, use the thick paste to sketch slimmer, pointier noses onto our faces. We rub a shimmery gold powder onto our cheekbones like they do in YouTube videos, TV commercials, magazines. Here, gimme. I said, GIVE IT TO ME! Never mind that our noses remain wide and flat, that the colors we dust onto our eyelids don't "pop," as promised; we do not realize they're shades meant for girls with fairer skin. Still, some of us are mesmerized with who we've become in mirrors. We touch our dewy cheeks and orb eyes. Others of us cannot stand the black gunk coating our eyelashes. We're only here because we don't want to miss anything. Our friends' fingers flutter over us. We bask in the warmth of their hands. In secret, hiding in bedrooms we've always shared, we unscrew bottles we've stolen from Rite Aid, CVS, Walgreens. We just want to try. We just want to see. We begin to paint our faces lighter, lighter. Until we are the color of lilies. Or bones. There. Beautiful.

LAST DAY

PROMISE EACH OTHER, AS WE RACE DOWN THE BOARD-walk beside our middle school, past Bagel Boy and O'Malley's Pub, the seagulls swooping low and cackling, that we will never grow apart. Lick popsicles that turn our lips blue: blue lips laughing, blue lips singing Mariah (*Your love's so good, I don't wanna let go-o-o-o*), blue lips puckered for a picture, smile! We step in and out of each other's shadows. Link arms. Promise to call me every day?

In September, we will begin high school. Some of our schools are scattered throughout the shinier parts of our borough—neighborhoods people *actually* refer to when they think of "Queens," far from the dregs we inhabit. Others of us are heading to Brooklyn, Manhattan, the Bronx. We have completed the process of applying to high schools, have ranked our desired schools from one to twelve, have finished months of test prep and taken city-wide admissions tests to earn seats at one of the eight public specialized schools in the city. We have interviewed and auditioned, have lugged instruments and portfolios to parts of the five boroughs we've never been. We have been evaluated, scored, judged. We do all this at the age of thirteen, already training ourselves in the competitive ways of the City That Never Sleeps. Our home. It is a process our parents, who weren't raised here, do not fully comprehend. But they let us go anyway. After all, the mantra *Education is the only way to succeed* is one our parents have carried from ancestral lands to this supposed Land of Opportunity. So, we board subways to unfamiliar neighborhoods. We go alone, but buoyed, full of excitement and possibility.

The most determined and headstrong of us have been accepted to high schools in Manhattan: Stuyvesant, Hunter, Beacon, to name a few. We are the ones who have gazed at the Manhattan skyline across the bay every single bus ride home, the ones who have longed for adventure, glamour, an escape from our neighborhoods, or all of the above. *Why do you have to go so far?* some of our loved ones asked. Others of us, pragmatic and straightforward, have chosen high schools in Queens. Townsend, Forest Hills, Cardozo, Francis Lewis, Adams. Why complicate things? We are the ones who could never leave these streets, nor the scent of the ocean, behind. We are content with the familiarity of our home borough, are thrilled and relieved to be in classes with our best friends. Because who would want to go to school with a bunch of stuck-up jerks from Manhattan, anyway?

However, in this moment, as we race down the boardwalk with two months of summer stretching before us, the future does not matter. We spend sticky July days together lounging on Rockaway Beach, ambling through the Museum of Natural History—sure, the dinosaur bones are cool but, more than this, the museum is air-conditioned and *donation-based,* which, to our fourteen-year-old ears means *free.* We head to the AMC in Times Square and buy one ticket each, which we use to sneak into three other movies. We stuff our faces with Sour Patch Kids and Raisinets as aliens from outer space transform into cars, a detective infiltrates people's dreams, and we watch the tenth remake of a superhero flick where the hero hails from Queens, like us. We throw popcorn at IMAX screens and each other. The buttery bits crunch between our teeth.

On a swampy August night, we meet at Gabby's and sing karaoke in her basement. Gabby's family has a machine, which includes a microphone coated with the spittle of many passionate singers, and a songbook with waxy beige pages. Gabby has the most beautiful voice of all of us, but never shows off, though we beg her. Together, we sing Britney, Christina, the Spice Girls, and even Abba and Celine Dion, whose songs we learned from our mothers and aunties. *Dancing queen! Young and sweet, only se-ven-teeeeen,* we screech, our voices inferior imitations of Abba but we don't care—we match them in spirit. When Gabby's older brother stomps down the stairs to steal slices from the pepperoni pizzas we'd ordered, we grow shy in his presence. But when he opens his mouth, says, *Y'all sound like a pack of hyenas,* we throw him out. We go back to singing Abba, allow ourselves to morph into our mothers. *Feel the beat FROM. THE. TAMBOURIIIIIINE!* Mostly, we spend our summer exploring the avenues and streets of our city together, occasionally stopping for snacks like sliced mangoes the color of sunshine and packaged in Ziploc bags, and churros with sugar that sink into our taste buds, sold from wire carts by brown women whose kind faces resemble our aunties'.

July, August, and early September pass this way, and we are happy in one another's company.

Two days before we are to begin our first day of high school, some of us bound for schools outside the dregs of Queens toss and turn in our beds. Words we've tried to forget resurface in our minds.

> *Isn't this neighborhood good*
> *enough for you, Michelle, Amalia,*
> *Sabina?*

What, you think you're better, Leah, Eun?

We squeeze our eyes tighter, pray for sleep to bury these voices. We fail.

> *Know-it-all. Arrogant.*

Don't expect a penny from me,

some of our mothers had said. In response to their words, we'd bitten our tongues, knowing it would be no use to take the bait. These arguments teach us that it is better to withdraw and keep our thoughts to ourselves. The hotheaded of us, however, shouted back, I DON'T WANT TO BE STUCK HERE FOREVER! and gestured to the greasy kitchen stoves, the faded couches, the fake, dusty plants, and china plates only used on special occasions (i.e., never). Houses—hidden, peripheral— our parents worked so hard to obtain.

The second these words flew from our mouths, we received slaps to our faces. Our cheeks stung. But before our mothers could take another hit, we turned away.

Because we cannot shake these memories from our heads, we get up. The clock reads 12:38 A.M.

What if they're right? we think. Why go far, why leave? It can't be too late to change our minds. We pick the crust from our eyes, dial each other's numbers. In whispered voices, we say, Are you up?

I am now, our friends—Desiree, Ruth, Victoria, Puja—grumble. What's the matter?

We say, Can we meet at Dunkin' in fifteen?

They pause. Huff. Fine.

We throw jackets over our mismatched pajamas, slip socked feet into sneakers. Shut the front door, slowly, slowly, so it doesn't make a sound. We rush six blocks, eleven minutes, toward the Dunkin' Donuts sign that twinkles in the distance like a neon North Star. Our friends arrive ten minutes later.

What the hell took so long? we hiss.

Sorry! I almost woke my little sister, and I heard my grandma praying in the bathroom.

We buy our friends a cruller, a glazed, a vanilla frosted donut with rainbow sprinkles, a hot chocolate. Shit, our friends say, that's my nosey-ass cousin at the register. Hide me! We huddle in the corner. Glance outside and spy a full moon. We turn back to their faces across sticky tables. How can faces alter so much, but change so little? we wonder. Our friends have chosen to remain in Queens, their schools thirty-minute bus rides away.

We explain everything: our families' hurtful words, the slaps to our cheeks no matter if we were silent or spoke up, the accusations of *You think you're better?* lodging in our heads, becoming doubts.

What if we fail? we say. What if our families are right about us? What if we're in way over our heads? What if—

Jesus! they interrupt. Don't let them get to you. You'll be great. We know you will.

At these last four words, we quiet. Bite into the glazed fried dough. We wipe our mouths with flimsy napkins.

Together, we walk down the Boulevard of Death. We pass the Exxon, the pharmacy, two pizzerias. We come to the block where our routes split. Hug each other tight, say, Text me when you get home.

PART TWO

WESTERN EPISTEMOLOGY

WE SIT IN HIGH SCHOOL CLASSROOMS, THE KINDS OF New York City public schools where metal detectors line entrances and American flags wave proudly above. Where during our lunch breaks strange men hang on chain-link fences, call, *Pssst! You! Hey, you! Come over here. I wanna tell you something.* When we realize they're speaking to us, we do not approach, though our stomachs churn in fear, disgust, and self-loathing. We've heard stories from our sisters and cousins, have watched reports on the nightly news, read headlines and articles, have been warned by our mothers, about men who lure girls, force themselves onto girls, rape girls, mutilate girls, leave girls, now dead, in suitcases on the side of highways or hidden in dumpsters to be found by somebody or nobody, men who keep girls as slaves for years so their families do not know whether they are alive or dead. *Three Women Discovered in 'House of Horrors'... Body of Missing Queens Woman Found in East River...* If not these explicit actions, we've heard about men who encroach upon girls in other, subtler ways.

Just last week, our cousins Yasmin, Shauna, Nancy, Carmen, Tamika, Rebekah, and Bernadette, also known as Bee, came home, their faces pale, and told their mothers, who told our mothers, who relayed their stories to us: Our cousins spoke of how strange men followed them after school and onto crowded subways. Placed their hands, without once looking at them, on our cousins' thighs and asses. How they unzipped their flies. How our cousins, on the verge of vomiting, fought to get off the train. How they turned around to look at these men's faces—Did that really happen?—only to hear their laughter. How that sound must have echoed in our cousins' ears as they took another route home. This is why some of us remain mute and still, say nothing to these men who hang on schoolyard fences, lest they fly into a rage. Invisibility will protect us, or so we believe. But others of us, livid and tired of keeping silent, fling our soda cans and foil wrappers with streaks of ketchup and greasy, empty bags of salt and vinegar chips at them. Orange liquid arcs through the air, splashes onto wire fences. FUCKING PERV! we shout at the tops of our lungs. Give these men the finger. Watch them scuttle away. But our rage does not banish our humiliation and fear, which we will never shake off, no matter how hard we try. Many of us, however, simply grit our teeth and turn away. We continue our conversations with our friends, Chanelle, Deepika, Ronnie, Lina. There's a party this coming weekend. *Pssst! You! Hey, you!* some men continue to call. Jesus, we say and roll our eyes. That asshole won't let up.

Some of us are placed in Freshman English Honors, where we learn words, and what a mouthful they are, words like *Western Epistemology* and *The Western Canon. The Pinnacle of Civilization*, etcetera, etcetera. But what exactly is The West? Are we The West? Is The West in us? We study Campbell's *Hero's Journey*, learn about the Greek gods, and the mythological male deities who morph into creatures—a white bull, a swan—in order to take, by cunning and manipulation, and when these methods fail, by force, what they want.

(In our nightmares, we come across suitcases rattling inexplicably. We approach, puzzled. Unzip them. They open like bodies cleaved in two. Contents: a swan, its elegant neck snapped, one deranged wing still beating. We don't remember our dreams when we wake.)

The next day, in English classes, we copy notes on Homer, Plato, Sophocles, Milton, and Dante, with care. We learn about Icarus flying too close to the sun. We read Shakespeare's sonnets addressed to his "dark lady."

My mistress' eyes are nothing like the sun . . . We wonder, But did she look like us? Was she as dark as us? But come on—

We don't look like anybody in these books. And nobody looks like us.

ART

SOME OF US (INCLUDING, BUT NOT LIMITED TO: ZAINAB, Nadine, Eva, Danielle, Odalis, Ellen, Sophie, and Aiza) travel from our homes—hidden, peripheral—to Lincoln Square, where, each day, we shuffle past the graceful stone buildings of the New York City Ballet, the Philharmonic, the Met Opera, and Juilliard to make our first classes at 8:05 A.M. Our public high school is renowned for its visual and performing arts programs, notorious for its three-hour-long auditions, which we'd spent months, if not years, unwittingly preparing for— We've sung in our church's choir, we've taken ballet lessons at the Y three times a week, and have stayed for free art classes offered after school each day.

Now we specialize in music, dance, drama, visual art, and even technical theater. We spend a minimum of four hours each day—which amounts to twenty hours per week, eighty hours per month, seven hundred and twenty hours per year, and two thousand eight hundred and eighty hours over the course of four years—in art classes. Advanced studio lessons include: Jazz Improv, Stanislavski Technique, Modern Dance, Oil Painting, Anatomy & Figure Drawing, Video Production. Cool and all, but outside of our workshops, this means we must also spend four years of our lives rolling our eyes at dance majors pirouetting atop lunch tables, drama students monologuing before answering questions in Pre-Calc, and instrumental music majors barging into class playing the intro to "Careless Whisper" by George Michael on their saxophones, *I'm never gonna dance again!* Actually, we don't mind this last bit too much; we bust out laughing and nearly piss our pants when our classmates start gyrating their hips. We are fifteen, and are learning to memorize the subway lines as if they are the very veins that run through our bodies.

At school, we learn things we're certain our parents don't know, never had the time to learn. For instance, we study the famous artists of the Renaissance. Michelangelo, Botticelli, Raphael, we recite. We jot down notes detailing sculptures, frescoes, and cathedrals while sitting in darkened AP Art History classes. Listen to the hundred-year-old slide projectors pop a sleepy *click click* with each rotation. We sketch self-portraits using charcoal that stains our fingertips for the rest of the week, or we opt for our favorite 4B pencils instead—We love the way the lead sluices the page like butter in a hot pan. We join our classmates and teachers to take customary, nerve-racking walks around enormous art studios to view everyone's work. When our teachers stop at our portraits, they remark, *It's all in the eyes,* and we watch our classmates nod in agreement. We bubble at their approval.

Some of us are voice majors, and we prepare ourselves to sing French and Italian arias by warming up our larynxes. *La la la LA la la laaaa!* Shift smoothly from one key to the next, higher and higher. We are sopranos, altos, prima donnas in training. *Open your mouths like this,* our teachers say. Dutifully, we reposition our tongues. Even in song, we become fluent in the language of our colonizers. Our English, impeccable. Our mother tongues, if we were taught them at all, become atrophied muscles, half-remembered melodies.

Our parents, who don't care for capital A *Art,* or *the pursuit of beauty,* or so we believe, say, *We don't understand, slow down, can you explain it again?* when they ask about our days. And when we see the confusion clouding their eyes, we feel powerful. Reckless. Mean.

NIGHT

BROWN GIRLS BROWN GIRLS BROWN GIRLS WHO SNEAK out basement doors and into cars that wait for them, engines idling, at the corner. Ruchi, Thanh, Victoria, Carmen, squeeze your asses in here! Damnit, Eva—your coat's stuck in the door. Hit the gas, Trish, a light just turned on in Sabina's house! Seriously, I don't know *how* you put on lipstick in the dark without a mirror, Rose. Practice, Rose grins. Chhhh, whatever, we say.

We drive to parties in neighborhoods where music blares from stereos all night long, and we listen as the reggae singer (Beenie Man?—No-o-o-o, it's Tanto Metro and Devonte! Felicia snaps) whines, *Everyone fal' in love sometime* ... Where one turns into two turns into five beers that spill onto kicks purchased from Nike and Steve Madden. We'd scrounged our babysitting and tutoring earnings, our profits from selling cupcakes on the sly at school, to buy them. We are sixteen. Brown boys' eyes roam our bodies. Some of us pretend not to notice, but hope they will come talk to us soon. Others of us straighten our shoulders and stare back, unflinching. This—our beauty—is the power we have. Or think we have. The braver boys respond, say, *Damn, you looking* mad *fresh.* We smile, kiss them on stoops as it snows. We let them hold our hands as they drive around the block, past the Dunkin' Donuts, the Dollar Tree, the Mobil gas station. When they park, we sit on their laps, and when we feel their desire, concentrated in the tightness of their jeans, we pull away. We say, You think I'm that easy? Or we whisper, Not here. Not now.

Some of us are, in fact, that easy. Easier than we thought. This comes to us as a shock—Does this mean we're *that* kind of girl now? We refasten our bras. But others of us shrug, unplagued by guilt. Whatever, we say, and after the deed, ask: Wanna split some fries, a pint of ice cream? All of us feel a new type of hunger, one that unfurls in our stomachs. We make love in unmade beds, on sofas, on floors. (What did it feel like? Did it hurt? Was it good? Did he have a big—? Some of us respond, I don't know if he had a big dick, I didn't fuck him. Though I can tell you she smelled *incredible,* like Cinnabons!— Oh shit! our friends squeal.) Lying naked after, we listen to the radio. Aaliyah croons, *Boy, I been watching you like a hawk in the sky . . .* When we feel a chill, we tug our sweaters over our heads. Others confess the truth to our friends: We hadn't fucked. The most we'd felt comfortable with was holding hands.

Think: brown plus brown equals brown. Brown plus brown equals never again. Equals sometimes, hit me up when you're in my hood. Equals nobody else but you. Equals take me home, I need to go home.

(*Tell me, are you that somebody?* Aaliyah asks.)

It doesn't cross our minds to consider what our parents might do if they caught us. We believe they won't. They're too busy, too exhausted, to notice. As a result, we grow bold, wild, we become adept liars. (Some of our parents, however, eventually discover our empty beds stuffed with pillows meant to resemble our sleeping bodies. They whoop our asses the next day and give us death glares for the next month. Some threaten to put bars on our windows, or send us back to India, the Philippines, Mexico, Jamaica, Ghana, the Dominican Republic. Some of them are merely bluffing, while others are serious.

(Others of us, though, when we return home, creep up staircases. We are greeted by voices in the dark. In response, we let out blood-curdling screams—we swear we're in the presence of ghosts. Until we come face-to-face with the women who birthed us. *Where have you been?* they ask, dead calm. Another mother, when she discovers us gone, simply goes to bed and does not mention it the next day. Or ever. She is the mother who already knows answers to questions she does not need to utter.)

We stay out until the sun begins to stretch over rooftops, until we tell our friends, We've got to leave, NOW!

At front doors, we dig into our purses. Hiss, Shit! Are you kidding me?! and we beg our siblings to let us in—Please just this one time!—because, in our rush to leave, we'd forgotten our keys.

BROWN BOYS

WE LOVE THEIR FLUFFY HAIR THAT HOUSES AFRO picks, their hair that's smooth and soft as silk, hair so dense our fingers get stuck, hair that, from its roots, gives the appearance of growing tamely, until the strands poke from the sides of their heads like porcupine quills, and cause us to giggle. We hug Jae, Malcolm, Sameer, David, Liang, Miguel, Juan, Feng, Jesse, and Omar—to name just a few—from behind. On tiptoe, we trace our tongues over lightning bolts barbers carefully buzzed onto their scalps, jagged points tapering just above their ears. Brown boys shiver, say, *Stop that, you weirdo.* They laugh. Brown boys who, we believe, are themselves lightning incarnate: flashes of startling beauty, possessing an equal ability to illuminate and destroy us. Leave us scorched and stunned. (Did you know, we tell them, that people have a greater

chance of getting struck by lightning *twice* than winning the lottery? But what, we wonder, as we walk beside brown boys, are our chances of winning the lottery
and getting struck by some force of nature?)

Brown boys loop their bodies around scaffolding,
jump to grasp the metal rods above their heads and do
pull-ups, and we roll our eyes. Show-offs, we mutter
(though we love to watch them). Brown boys brush
their fingertips against cool stone walls in Central Park
before gracefully arching into backflips—Gravity, for
them, knows no bounds. Brown boys break-dance, tum-
ble and spin, beside the Brooklyn Bridge. Tourists toss
dollar bills into brown boys' hats. Brown boys wait for us
outside subway stations, don massive headphones and
baggy jeans. We greet them hello with a kiss. If they're
extra cheesy, they say, *I got you something,* and present
us with a single long-stemmed rose.

Today, we've decided to walk through Prospect Park.
We meet them on the Flatbush Avenue side, pick up
beef patties and scarf them down before our walk. We
dust the crumbs from our chins. Together, we amble
along the park's trails with no particular destination in
mind. We glance at the patchy grass littered with candy
wrappers and empty soda bottles with dumb names like
West Indian Queen. As we continue to walk, the terrain
morphs into petunias planted in orderly rows. We see
white women jogging, their terriers bobbing beside them.
Stately brownstones and cafés line the blocks. Here, we

do not notice a single piece of trash in sight. From these details, we deduce we've crossed into the "safe" side of the park. One white woman, when she passes us, pulls her purse closer to her fleshy hip. We grasp our brown boys' hands, feel their warmth. We keep our eyes ahead, half-listen as they point out an eagle. Hear her murmur, *Thank God they stick to their own kind.*

YOUR OWN KIND

T'S NOT THAT WE'RE RACIST, OUR PARENTS SAY. THEN WHAT IS it? we ask. *It's just. We don't want you dating* those *kinds of boys.* Which kinds of boys? we say, pressing them to be specific, although we already know which "kinds" they're referring to. Our parents do not answer us, so we try another route. Why can't we date them? we say. *Well, it'd be best if you dated your own kind.* Or, they say, *If you didn't date your own kind.* (What?) *They're not faithful—look at your Auntie Mia and Edith and Tasha whose husbands took a second wife behind their backs. Look at Auntie Charlene and Virginia and Sadya—Remember how their marriages ended?* (And our own fathers? we want to ask, but bite our tongues.) *Think of your cousin Myra, Jade, and Cristina. They divorced after just two years! Those men,* our families say, *are aggressive. They drink too much and gamble their money away and never come home and who knows where they'll be. They're unreliable, violent.* Our parents add, *Aren't you scared?* Scared of what? we ask. Tess, Linh, Maheen—remember her?—introduced us. He wants to be an architect, a doctor, a filmmaker, a chef. He's sweet, we say. *They're too different.* And finally, *Those boys are beneath you—do you not see?*

And so, some of us—the obedient girls, the never-let-down-your-family girls, the don't-you-want-something-better-for-yourselves? girls—do "see." We force ourselves to believe that these boys are beneath us, despite the fact that the difference between our skin tones is but a few shades. We do our best to avoid them as we slink down school hallways, ignore their phone calls and texts, their notes slipped into our lockers or handed to us by mutual friends, which we do not read.

When we run into them on the Boulevard of Death, we rush across the crowded street. Some of us, however, are unable to slip past them. Brown boys stop us with a firm *Hey.* We cringe when we meet their confused faces. We cross our arms and hunch our shoulders and try to shrink ourselves. In that moment, we long to run and hide, while others of us want to stay, open our mouths and explain our disappearance from their lives. But what explanations could we possibly give?

We say nothing.

Others of us long to place our hands on their cheeks, but when we do, brown boys dodge our touch. Shame wells within us, a feeling we will carry in our bones for the rest of our lives when this memory resurfaces, unbidden, in our minds.

Yet, others of us, during this brief encounter, notice details we hadn't registered before: brown boys' dirty sneakers, their unruly hair, the rip in their jeans from running wild through Manhattan when they should've been composed. Decent. We observe these details and brim with disgust. Our eyes bore into theirs until they are nothing to us, until we stop caring about what they think and how they feel, which makes it easier for us to let them go. We turn our backs, ignore their questions. We head home. When we reach our brick houses—hidden, peripheral—we wash our hands. Splash water onto our cheeks, our necks, until we feel an urge to scrub every inch of our bodies. We stumble into showers, blast the hot water until it scalds our skin. Turn the knob until the water becomes so cold our teeth chatter.

On the phone with our friends that evening—Guess who I saw on the boulevard? Man, he was pathetic!—we practice slimming our noses with makeup. We have grown skilled in the art of dissembling.

Our faces, in mirrors, smile back.

EVERYTHING WE EVER WANTED

SEVENTEEN. WHITE BOYS TOUCH OUR SKIN. *BEAUTIFUL,* they say. Together, we lie on Central Park's springy grass and ride rented bikes across the fart-smelling East River. Just to be near them feels like we are coveting something precious (diamonds that now belong to us). Never mind that we also feel as if our skin was smeared with dirt. We do our best to ignore this. When we pass cars parked on the streets, we catch fleeting views of our warped reflections: our noses stretched like Pinocchio's, our mouths, the width of needles. We turn away quickly, though white boys do not notice. Their reflections, by contrast, are glossy and tower over us. Think: Do we look like prostitutes beside them? Do we remind them of their nannies and maids, their favorite porn stars? (*SHHH! Don't. Say. A. Single. Word!*)

Lighten up! we tell ourselves. We are young! The sun glistens on our faces.

White boys take us to their homes in Midtown, the Upper East Side, Tribeca, the West Village, where we enter buildings we've strolled past but never imagined setting foot in. We make our way through marble lobbies and are greeted by doormen dressed in overcoats and funny hats, like in the movies. When they smile at us, we realize that they resemble our uncles, our brothers. All we can do is smile in return.

We enter apartments where abstract paintings in gold frames are hung on walls, and private schools with names like Nightingale and Spence and Trinity, and villas in Tuscany and cabins in Aspen and beach houses off the coast of Maine are offhandedly discussed. Where, during dinner, their siblings sigh and say, *I don't know— Princeton or Harvard?* (They will not get into either.) In their homes, we smile and nod and mask ourselves behind laughs that we believe are elegant, until we hear the sound stream from our lips, grate against our ears. HA HA HA HA. We clamp our jaws shut, quick. We are here to meet their parents. *Charming!* their parents call us. *Your friend is SO charming.*

During our dinner of grass-fed meats and oven-roasted vegetables purchased from farmers markets and imported cheeses from lands we hope to travel to one day—white boys and their families have already been, of course—we suddenly become Ambassadors of Third World Nations. Their fathers and mothers ask: *What do you think is the root cause of poverty in your country? Excuse me, your parents' country. What are the ways the dictatorship—oh, it's awful, isn't it?—might fold? What do you think of NAFTA?*

We swallow. Dried bits of free-range chicken inch down our throats.

Brown girls brown girls brown girls who morph into marionettes on a stage—*Charming, so charming!*—spotlights hot and blinding.

After dinner, white boys take us to their rooftops overlooking the Empire State Building, the World Trade Center. Note, however: If white boys are not rich and/or WASP-y, if, instead of lawyers and surgeons and financiers and trust-fund inheritors, their parents are sales supervisors for corporations or clerks for the city or middle school English teachers (see: *middle class*), or if their parents are construction workers or secretaries (see: *lower-middle class*), the details we observe will be slightly different, of course: replace "Harvard" with state schools like "Albany" or "Binghamton," and city universities like "Brooklyn," "Baruch." Replace "organic roasted veggies" with "spaghetti" or "pizza." Replace "rooftop" with "marina," the "Empire State Building" and "World Trade Center" with the "Statue of Liberty," or the oh-so-scenic "Belt Parkway."

Replace the questions, "What do you think is the root cause of poverty in your country?" with accounts of how their families fought in the Korean, Vietnam, Gulf wars, and, these days, against *those terrorists* in Afghanistan and Iran.

No matter their class, politely correct them when they interchange Singapore for the Philippines, Colombia for the Dominican Republic, Haiti for Jamaica. They go on, *I don't understand why it's frowned upon these days to build a wall at the border of Mexico—I mean, there ARE legal ways of coming to this country.* They say, *Aren't your parents frustrated by those illegals getting a free pass, breaking the law?*

Because some of us are desperate to be accepted by their families, thus, extremely impressionable (they could tell us to jump off the Verrazano and we'd do it; they could tell us Christ's Second Coming was tomorrow, and we'd repent of all our sins)—we nod vehemently in agreement, quick to forget our own undocumented loved ones in Queens.

No matter their zip code or tax bracket, listen as these white people deem us and our families the *good immigrants,* the *hard-working ones—not like the lazy people in this country who are a burden on the system.* (It dawns on us that some of our families have parroted these arguments, too.) No, we are the *grateful brown people.* Thank you for colonizing our ancestors' countries, for the wars and dictators! We are so thankful for your *civilizing* religion and visas! Oh thank you, thank you, thank you.

Still, no matter which details you replace, keep the sentiment—that we are outsiders—the same.

Rooftops, piers, the Belt Parkway—wherever the fuck we are, we cannot glimpse our neighborhood from this distance. It is practically nonexistent.

Illuminated by the moonlight, we glow darker.

Beautiful, white boys call us, again. They run their hands over our necks and shoulders. *You know that, right?*

For some of us, this affirmation is what we've been dying to hear our entire lives. We bask in their words, feel a validation we've never felt before. Others of us merely purse our lips, give a tight smile—We don't believe them when they call us gorgeous and, for the rest of our lives, will always feel unease in rooms filled with white people, no matter how friendly.

A few others of us simply look at white boys. A rude sound punctures the air—a snort that bubbles, we realize, from the backs of our throats. It grows into a force that spills from our guts and causes us to double over. We cannot help it. *Beautiful, you know that, right?* Clutching our stomachs, the night rings with our real laughter— uninhibited, wild—until we can no longer breathe. We lean on the edges of rooftops, on bridges where cars zoom beneath us, and marinas where the ocean roils, waves choppy, each flap of water like leaping hands ready to pull us in. We are so close we could fall. And what if we did?

Brown girls, grown girls, brown girls. We have never felt more alone.

Some white boys, confused by our sudden outburst, recoil, take a step back. Others hesitate before joining in, unaware that we're laughing at them and their lame-ass dinners and apartments, their stupid families, and, most of all, our stupid selves.

Other white boys—Jack, Aaron, Brad, John, Jake—look at us. As if seeing us for the first time. They're silent when they catch our gaze. They lean in with an embrace whose gentleness startles us. Some of us stiffen—We don't want to be touched, we push them away. Others of us let their arms encircle our bodies—We give in. Some of us, we realize with a jolt, *do* want to be held, and anyone will do.

From a bird's-eye view, observe: bodies in a city so bright, you cannot see the stars.

TERRITORY

T'LL BE FUN, WE SAY, AND WE TAKE OUR WHITE BOYS ON A trip to Queens. We've grown tired of spending our days and dollars hanging in *the city*—that is, Manhattan. As if it were the only part of the five boroughs that existed. We've come to despise the people who elbow us as they speed down sidewalks, we roll our eyes at the overpriced cafés and restaurants dubbed *très chic* and *edgy* because, we realize, they're slumming it (mimosas and avocado toast paired with crumbling brick walls). We laugh at the women dressed in ugly designer clothing, standing on corners, trying to hail cabs.

When we ride subways in *the city*, we note how they're air-conditioned, with neat electronic maps that indicate the ease of traveling from point A to B, as well as how these lines never break down in Manhattan like they do in our home borough—and why the fuck is that? (*Ladies and gentlemen, this train is now running on the local track. This train will be rerouted over the bridge and will skip the following ten stops. This train is delayed because of a signal malfunction at Eightieth Street. Because of a sick passenger. Because of a police investigation at Broadway Junction. Attention! This train is out of order and is no longer running. Please take the shuttle bus instead—Enjoy the rest of your day!*) We've grown tired of Manhattan's "glamour," which, like the knockoff Coach bags sold on Canal Street and the Botoxed faces on the Upper East Side, is, in reality, fake as hell.

So instead, we take our white boys to our home turf. From subways we watch high-rises transform to squat buildings and bodegas. We point out city hospitals—Elmhurst, Jamaica, Woodhull—where we were born, where some of our parents work as janitors, aides, nurses, social workers, paper pushers. We stroll past a supermarket with boxes of tomatoes, avocadoes, pineapples, and other produce stacked neatly out front. A ripped plastic bag, a used napkin wafts toward us. We bat it away.

This is the playground where we'd chill with our brothers and sisters, we tell white boys. We touch the monkey bars dull from children's hands. Around us, a cacophony of

Hoy, pare! Kumusta?

你好嗎?

¡Prima! ¿Qué lo que?

آپ کیسے ہیں؟

Bạn khỏe không?

Our ears are trained to hear them. *Look at this place!* our white boys say. Sauntering along sidewalks, we hold our white boys' hands. (Or maybe they are the ones clinging on to us?) We pass a little boy walking with his abuela, dressed in a Spider-Man costume, even though it isn't Halloween.

Hear the *shuh shuh* sound of brown boys' sneakers playing basketball. Feet blurred, swift as wind. Brown boys say, *Hey—what's good?* and toss their chins up at us. Ignore the white boys at our sides. Fresh, you look-ing mad fresh, their eyes say. Some of the boys simply stop, ball in hand, as we walk by. *Yo! When you over him, you know where I'm at!* We hear them laugh, high-five their friends, and we blush, drag our white boys away. *Coconut!* they call after us. *Uncle Tom! Banana! Bitch!*

No matter, we think, as we walk away with our prize. *What an asshole,* our white boys say. *What was that about?*

But some of these brown boys, when we pass them,

call us by our names. Not our American names, but our names spoken in cramped living rooms, ones used by our grandmothers to shake us awake. They call us by our names, our names like tiny flowers, and when we hear them, we must do our very best to walk away.

OUR MOTHERS SPEAK

G ROW UP. GO TO SCHOOL. GET MARRIED. HAVE KIDS. *Work, work, and work some more until you die. That's it—what else is there?* Our mothers bestow their wisdom to us in kitchens once painted a sunshine yellow, now faded, in bathrooms where they brush their hair beneath fluorescent lights and pause when they come upon gray strands that they swiftly, expertly pluck from their scalps. They convey their wisdom to us while they zip up our satin prom dresses, and when we lie on musty couches, beat, dreaming of him after a night we'd slipped out. They gift us with their insight when, at last, we receive college acceptance letters (*I am delighted to inform you . . .*). Our mothers call our names—Ximena, Kim, Hema, Nadira, Krystel, Usha, Truc, Nazreen, Meiying, and our nicknames, too—say, *Are you listening? It's a cycle.* Yawning, they glance at clocks. Inside we shrivel a little. Shrug to the left in order to escape our mothers' fingers that hover over the clasps of our undone dresses. Our mothers stand behind us and seek our gazes in mirrors. Our not-reflections. *Are you listening?* they repeat. We do not answer them. Instead we busy ourselves, run the tap over their voices or, better yet, blast hair dryers. Chop peppers and carrots atop oil-flecked tables. Say nothing, absolutely nothing at all, but think: Wrong.

OUR MOTHERS' COMMANDMENTS

Command #1

You shall not be a troublesome girl, the kind who disagrees and doesn't know how to be quiet. You shall be a good girl. Sweet, compliant. Obey, for I am the Lord your Mother, and I brought you into this world.

Command #2

You shall not be an ugly girl. Do not spend hours in the sun, lest your already dark skin grows darker. Be a Lady, with a pretty smile and a pretty face. Look how your hair is limp and dry, your lips chapped, like a ghost! Look at your lipstick with its too-bright shade, how your purse is ratty and frayed. Change your sinful ways and make them pleasing unto me, says the Lord your Mother.

Command #3

You shall not be a loud girl, with many opinions. Yes, I know you are intelligent—after all, I raised you—but it's unbecoming to broadcast your smarts. Instead, be a quiet girl. One who clears the table, sweeps the floor, washes the dishes, does the laundry. Do not argue. Submit, for I am the Lord your Mother, and I created you.

Command #4

You shall not be a wayward girl, with many lovers. Do not ask about birth control—why would you need birth control? Do not get pregnant.* Decent girls do not think about sex.

Command #5

You shall not be a rebellious girl. Instead, always follow these rules, including the many not listed here. Commands you must store in your bones, your every movement. Obey, for I am the Lord your—

What do you mean you don't remember what those other rules are? Have I taught you nothing?!

* See cousins Sidra, Evangeline, Camilla, Ashanti, Mercedes, Jocelyn, and Aarti for what *not* to do.

GREAT EXPECTATIONS

OUR BROTHERS—WHOSE DNA WE SHARE, WHOSE EYES also crinkle when they smile, who've grown up in the same households, who raise their bikes high into the air, silhouetted only by the blue sky—piss off their old-lady teachers. When they are released from the dean's office, we sit cross-legged beside them on basketball courts. We've cut our last classes of the day—AP U.S. History, Calculus AB, gym—to meet up with them. They smoke and sometimes we join them. Where'd you get this? we ask, and gesture to the joint in hand. *Does it matter?* We shrug, inhale, feel the vapors gather in our chests, the sticky, metallic flavors that settle onto our tongues. Release.

Sometimes, we don't smoke. We just sit and listen. *One day, I'm getting out of here*, our brothers say. *Far away. What do you think it's like in Wyoming?* What, we laugh, you want to be a cowboy? *I've been thinking—maybe I'll join the military. Why not? GI Bill, free college.* They toss sideways glances our way. *Not that you need to worry about college money.* We shrug, nonchalant. Some of us have received merit scholarships and full rides to attend universities. Our sleepless nights and commutes spent studying for AP classes have paid off. When we hung out at some of our white friends' houses, though, we didn't know how to respond when their parents slipped in a *You know, Madeline's grades were excellent, but I suppose all the schools she was rejected from had to fill their quota for certain students this year.* Certain students? Did we hear that right? Our faces burned in anger, confusion, and shame.

Meanwhile, in our own hoods, we've learned to downplay our smarts. At the sight of our report cards listing straight A's, our sketchbooks, the stack of novels and comics from the library we're forced to carry in our arms because we cannot fit them into our backpacks (they're for our history papers and to read at night), after our arriving home, spent, from two-hour-long commutes from high schools in Manhattan and the shinier parts of our borough, some family members and friends meet us with accusations of *What—you think you're better? See, she's too haughty to even look us in the eye!* they say, when we stare at the ground, shocked and hurt by their words. We have been admonished to *Study hard!* yet have also been told *Don't go far, stay close, stay near, aren't we good enough for you?* We long for more, but keep our dreams to ourselves. Our brothers, on the other hand, announce, *I'll do a cross-country trip on a motorcycle. I'll work in a casino in Vegas. I'll drive to Mexico and sip mezcal all day. I'll head west and make bank. But first,* they tell us, *I'll do some construction gigs, save money, then jet.* But you're smart enough to construct the goddamn building! we protest. *It's not about that,* they say. *I just want to get out. I'm going to get out.* We make the mistake, in that moment, of believing them.

THIRST

JOHNNIE WALKER ON ICE! A DOUBLE SHOT! SHOUT OUR swaggering fathers and uncles, red-faced, brimming. Bursting. How we love them. We must try hard not to bust out laughing when they belt out national anthems to countries that aren't the U.S. of A. Our fathers and uncles, who are as familiar as they are mysterious to us, mix Absolut and orange juice, crush Budweiser cans, pour homemade wine into chipped mugs, concocted from recipes hailing from lands we've never been to or can only dimly recall. We sneak into backyards with flimsy fences where our fathers and uncles toast Jameson and smoke cigarettes, hookah, and ganja on a night when winter is beginning to loosen its grip and let spring bloom. We pretend to pour ourselves Pepsi and orange soda, as we cough and slyly swipe a bottle of Grey Goose from the table. Upstairs, our cousins lie in wait. *Try to grab the Patrón, too! You know they can't handle that shit.* Our fathers and uncles shout, *Here's to fucking-over that bastard Duvalier, Marcos, Trujillo! To leaving that hell-hole, quick!* Stories, always stories, of the men, versions of themselves, they left behind. When they were history and chemistry professors, cardiologists and internists, engineers who constructed bridges and roads in countries oceans away. Our fathers and uncles, however, don't talk about their bosses now. Except to mimic their supervisors' voices, consonants crisp and assured. They put extra bass into their voices and switch, of course, to English. *Tell me,* they mime. *Is it true that your people practice voodoo? That your women are gold diggers? That your people eat dog?*

We tiptoe through living rooms and kitchens in order to reach bedrooms where our cousins are surely growing antsy. On our way, we hear laughter whose pitch threatens to shatter our eardrums. Not Johnnie or Absolut for our mothers and aunties, who cover their mouths when they laugh, gold bangles clinking, but Cabernet Sauv, which streaks the inner flesh of their lips mulberry. Margaritas, if they're feeling festive or homesick. And always Prosecco for the lightweights like Auntie Dolores who moans, *Thirty-seven! My daughter's thirty-seven and hasn't dated anyone in five years— I'll never have a grandchild!* If our mothers and aunties drink at all—and not all of them do, for some view the act as unseemly or immoral—they drink away from their men. Away from us. And, by separating themselves, re-main pure, motherly. They sing Rihanna, *Shine bright like a diamond! Ha ha ha ha. My,* they say as they catch sight of us slinking up the carpeted staircase. Fuck, we mutter. Turn around. *You're really blossoming into a young lady!* they say. Uh, right, we say. Blossoming.

We fumble with the bottles stuffed under our sweat-shirts bearing the names of the colleges we will attend in the fall. Some of us wear hoodies that announce Stony Brook and New Paltz, state schools that we have the good fortune of escaping to. Most of us, however, don the names of city universities: Hunter, City, John Jay (whose glossy brochures exclaimed, *The best bang for your buck!,* which pleased our parents). We will com-mute from our homes in the dregs of Queens to cam-puses in the fall. Few of us are branded with private school names. If we are, they're colleges that are also located in our home city or not too far away, on Long Island: Fordham, Hofstra, and one shining Columbia. From the staircase where we're eye-level with the fake chandelier, sweat pools on our upper lips. We pray the bottles hidden in our sweatshirts do not clink together and reveal our mission.

Tell us, do you have a boyfriend now? Which college are you going to again? You're studying premed, finance, management, right?

We do not mention our boyfriends or girlfriends (it's a trick question), or how one of us is slowly coming to terms with being gay, how others of us are looking forward to college where we will experiment with winged eyeliner despite our deeper voices, or newly shorn hair slicked back with pomade, to mirror the way our brothers style themselves.

Our aunties say, *Don't go too far. Stay here. Stay close.* We watch them pat their breasts and stomachs, their dyed roots. Some of our aunties and mothers pour shots of tequila, but do not offer us one. From staircases, we watch them toss back their heads, and we imagine the alcohol, the way it burns their throats as they swallow. It's the same satisfying sensation we will soon feel with our cousins, if only we could get to them. (It's too early in the night to realize a different, but related, burn will rush up our esophagi on car rides home. The kind that will force us to stick our heads from minivan windows, where we will momentarily be soothed by the winter wind caressing our faces. Until the moment passes, and our stomachs lurch once more. We wretch. Huh—HUH! Our fathers, witnessing us from drivers' seats [they've sobered up, ish, with two cups of coffee], begin to shout. *This child of mine!* But when they pull over, enraged, they begin to gag, too. Ha ha ha ha. Like father like—)

In this particular moment, however, glass bottles heavy beneath our hoodies, we observe our mothers and aunties take shots, chomp into lime wedges. Mouths pinched, they shake their heads from side to side, shudder, *Sour! Ach, sour!*

PART THREE

WELCOME TO MARS!

SOME OF US LEAVE ANYWAY. FOR UNIVERSITIES—BERKELEY, Northwestern, UT Austin—across the country. Sayonara, New York! we say, I'm fucking outta here! and we are not the least sad to go. A few of us head to our city's Ivy League university dozens of subway stops—practically light-years—away. We arrive in parts of the country, or a neighborhood in our own city, the Big Apple, that we have no previous knowledge of. Whose campus features architecture straight from our AP Art History textbooks ("Chapter 12: The Revival of Greek and Roman Classical Antiquity & the Birth of Neoclassicism"), where lawns are perfectly mowed and even the garbage cans shine. Looking around, we are certain there has been a mistake, a mix-up in admissions. We know we don't belong here.

Our schedules: Introduction to Modern Biology, Principles of Economics, Programming in Java, Statistical Reasoning. Classes that make our parents proud. In seminars, we are privy to our classmates' conversations. *My trip to Ibiza was crazy!* they say. *From there, we chartered a plane to Monaco, then Santorini.* We sit between an oil mogul's daughter and some guy whose dad is a Fortune 500 exec. We listen to our classmates say, *Well, my grandfather, father, and brother all went to this college—but besides that, I REALLY didn't have a leg up.* Try not to roll our eyes to the back of our heads.

During our lunch breaks, we chill on the library's steps (it is one of the university's two dozen libraries) and soak up the late-September sun. From our perch, which overlooks campus, we ponder the word "legacy." Think: How many people simply bought their way into these Ivy League institutions where tuitions are equal to, or greater than, the annual income of households in our neighborhood?

Legacy.

Our families' legacies, the histories we've inherited: grandparents who never learned to read, U.S.-backed dictatorships, bombs, wars, refugee camps, naval bases, canals, gold, diamonds, oil, missionaries, brain drain, the American Dream.

Where'd you go to high school? we ask our classmates when we learn that they, too, are native New Yorkers. We listen as they compare boarding schools in the Berkshires and other New England locations that conjure, in our minds, landscapes filled with trees and castlelike dorms. The kinds of picturesque places, we think, that are settings to movies where everyone gets murdered.

But why did you have to go to boarding school? we ask. This prompts our classmates' laughter. *Oh, Aditi, Alexandra, Puja, Mercedes!* they say, though some of them pronounce our names wrong. We don't bother correcting them. *You're so funny!*

Some of our classmates we like. But most, we don't.

Still, we force ourselves to laugh along with them, knowing our families have cleaned their apartments, picked up their dogs' shit, raised them and all their siblings. Or, if our parents were "better off," cared for their relatives in hospitals as nurses, aides, therapists. *Excuse me, Mr. Van der Deen, is there anything I could get for you? Mr. Van der Deen, I noticed you rang your bell several times? Oh, Mr. Van der Deen, please, no need to yell!*

Like ghosts, we wander the edges of campuses. We pass the sculpted, lush hedges and the cherry blossom trees with their delicate branches that flank the perimeter. Just beyond the foliage, however, if we look carefully, we can glimpse the wrought iron gates that hem us in. A desire to escape, to run far away, overcomes us. But we are good girls—we force ourselves to stay. Because we are the ones who've "made it," haven't we? We're the ones who have worked *so hard.* American girls living the American Dream.

But for what? And for who?

We find ourselves standing before a statue. Beneath the monument's sturdy sandaled toes chiseled from stone, a plaque reads: PLATO——FOUNDER OF THE ACADEMY, THE FIRST INSTITUTION OF LEARNING IN THE WESTERN WORLD. A cold wind sweeps past us. Shoulders hunched, we wrap our coats closer to our bodies.

REUNION

IVE STELLAS, PLEASE. ACTUALLY, HOW ABOUT A ROUND OF mojitos? I haven't seen ya'll in *ages*. No, don't listen to her—One bottle of the Sancerre, the one from the Loire Valley. Damn, look at you, Miss Fancy! Oooh, that waiter was cute, wasn't he? Kinda looked like Aiza's brother— Ugh, barf, says Aiza, *Please* stop talking. We cackle and settle on different drinks—one Riesling, one lychee martini, one peach soju, one vodka and ginger ale, one Jack Daniels, neat (Who are you, my uncle?)— but end up sipping from each other's glasses throughout the night. Just one taste, we say. It's been so long. How are you, girl? Only when we are around each other can we let our performances drop. I'm so fucking tired, we say, without having to explain. I'm just so tired. Our litany of complaints: At this stupid party I went to— and I knew I should've left once I heard that whack-ass music—dudes kept asking me where I was "from." I had them guess each time. I swear to God, I ended up saying, I'm from the tropical land of Queens, you dumbasses. One girl had the nerve to ask whether Queens was "dangerous." Can you believe that shit? So just to fuck with her and the rest of them, I looked her dead in the eye and said, Well, I guess I *could* cut you now. (Yo-o-o, we say, laughing. That's OD.) We were reading this story in my Lit class, right? The main character's this Black woman. Tell me WHY my professor turned to me and was like, *Well, Angelique, how do* YOU *feel about this representation?* I nearly *slapped* her, let me tell you. Hey, that's better than in middle school when those assholes in class, Joseph Justin and them, called me a terrorist for a whole year, says Jamila. Alright, y'all, get this: This girl from my psych class? I kid you not, she came up to me one day and said (here, we pinch our noses to mimic her nasally voice), *It must be* soooo *hard being—* And I said, Being what? Bitch, I *dare* you to finish that sentence.

JENNY

OUR STATISTICS PROFESSOR ASKS: *HOW MANY STANDARD deviations does this point fall from the mean?* as our eyes wander from the whiteboard crammed with equations and graphs to the curve of Jenny's shoulders, her thighs, and lips. *If B = the sound of her laughter, and C = the number of times her face appears, without warning, in our dreams, then solve for A, the frequency she enters our waking minds.* We want to be the ripped jeans she is wearing. Closer, closer. When we hug her hello after our lecture, we smell her green apple lotion. Her itchy sweater tickles our arms, and her curly hair brushes our cheeks. We close our eyes, inhale.

When we were nine, we kissed a friend at a slumber party, first as a dare, and then once more before bed to "practice." When we were fourteen, we stole our brothers' laptops, found links to sites we never knew existed, our eyes widening at the sight of breasts that made our stomachs flutter. We've crushed on the barista at the coffee shop, the one who never asked our names, but knew our orders as soon as we walked through the doors. *One matcha latte, one cortado with oat milk, one plain ol' Americano with a splash of half-and-half, coming right up!* We've fallen in love with the stranger we saw every other day at the library. Who snuck in a donut once, and when she'd finished, we fought the urge to wipe the dot of powdered sugar from the corner of her lips.

We are girls who braid our long hair, who wrap our locs at night. Who shave it all off with trembling hands and run our palms over our bristly scalps afterward. Can we be girls without gender? we wonder. Maybe we can ... No matter. When we excavate ourselves, we feel a freedom we've never known, one that will define the remainder of our lives. A freedom that must be fought for each day, as headlines read: *New FBI Hate Crimes Report Shows an Increase in Anti-LGBTQ Attacks.* When Jenny tells us she likes our new look, we blush. We tell her, You look bomb, too. But what we really want to say is, I love you, I love you, I— Shhh! Don't. Say. A. Single. Word.

In cathedrals where stained glass windows depict Mother Mary weeping over Jesus and filter in shards of colorful light, in mosques made of yellow brick, ripe with the scent of hard-working feet, in temples where the matches keep snapping in half whenever we try to light a stick of incense, while Buddha with his half-closed, sleepy eyelids smiles down at us—*What's wrong with you today?* our grandmothers ask—some of us are too frightened to pray. It's nothing, Grandma, we say, and squeeze her hand. We wonder if God will accept our prayers. (*God, please give me a body I can love. God, please help me have the strength to tell my family. God, please give me wings so I can leave this place behind.*) If we pray at all. Good "girls," we are good girls.

DUTY

THE MOST DUTIFUL OF US PASS ANATOMY & PHYSIOLOGY I and II, Organic Chemistry, Micro, Patho, Pharmacology, and make it to Clinical Rotations. Finish line! We are almost nurses, physical therapists, physician assistants. (Very few of us are doctors in training. *Too much school,* our mothers had said when some of us timidly asked their permission. *Too expensive.*) We train at Jamaica Hospital, Elmhurst Hospital, SUNY Downstate. Where addicts, drunks, and people riddled with scabs on their veins do not call us by our names. *Where's that Punjabi bitch? I said I didn't want a Black nurse treating me. Get the fuck out of my room. Get me a nurse who speaks English,* they say. *Not some FUCKING ching-chong.* We straighten our scrubs speckled with other people's blood and shit. Our calves burn from scurrying from body to body all night. *A career in healthcare is the best you could have,* our mothers, medical professionals themselves for twenty-five, thirty years, assured us. *Plus, I'm not paying for any other degree.* Obey. Our fellow trainees inject patients with morphine, heave a diabetic man into bed, sponge vomit from a drunk's chin. While we nonchalantly step into the janitor's closet wedged between room 6B and a vending machine. *Code Blue, Dr. Roberts to the ER, Code Blue,* we hear on the intercom, just outside the door. Our tears, pathetic and hot, slide down our cheeks. A practical, safe job for a dutiful daughter.

But the most reckless, headstrong—and truthful— of us abandon all pretenses after our second semester report cards expose our mediocrity:

```
Principles of Economics = C-
Programming in Java = D-
Modern Biology = D-
Statistical Reasoning = F
```

We've received official letters informing us that we *do not meet the minimum GPA requirement for the Honors College and will now be placed on Academic Probation.* We are warned: *Any future semester with a GPA below the minimum will be grounds for dismissal.* Fuck you, too, we mutter, and crumple the embossed letterheads in our fists. (Uncrumple, read them again.) We sink into our beds, knowing our parents will crush us.

After two weeks, we shrug off our comforters, which are in desperate need of a wash, step over bowls crusted with streaks of dried ice cream. Shower. Dispense with our potato odor, but not our funk. To cheer the fuck up, we take the subway to the MoMA, the Met (our elective, Studio Art: Painting = A). Find comfort in Dali's melting clocks, Van Gogh's nauseating sunflowers, fall into the void that is the man's mouth in Munch's *The Scream*, stare, mesmerized, at planes of indigo against brown in Rothko's *No. 61 (Rust and Blue)*. We catch the subway to West 4th, head to the indie theater, IFC, across the street from McDonald's and a basketball match taking place on the weathered court. Glimpse the sweat on the players' foreheads as they dart and pivot, slam dunk. At IFC, we buy tickets to the Miyazaki films playing marathon-style. We dab our eyes when Chihiro remembers the river spirit's name and sets him free. After, we find spots on benches in Washington Square Park next to a man in a tutu and an NYU student offering a poem, a free poem. We fill the empty pages of our microeconomics notebooks with sketches. We walk to the Strand, climb a ladder to reach *1984* at the top of a ten-foot-tall bookcase. *It's dope*, our brothers said. We pay $8.62 for a used copy. Devour the novel in one night.

The next day, with a sleep-deprived faculty advisor as our witness, we declare Art our major. (*You did what?!* our brothers shout, when we tell them on the phone, jackhammers and electric drills ramming concrete in the background.)

Art, our savior, our vanquisher—no, vessel—of funk.

Call our fathers, mothers. Give them the news. *Art?* they say. *But how will you eat? And how could you shame us like this?* They hang up before we have a chance to explain (not that explanations would matter). We stand on fire escapes outside our dorms at Hunter, Fordham, St. John's, Columbia. We have not gone far. Carefully, we drop our notebooks into the dumpsters below. Exhale. Feel as if we've woken from a bad dream.

OUR BROTHERS

New York State Record of Arrest and Prosecution
Criminal Charges:

1 —NY Penal Law §220.16: Possession with intent to
distribute (PWID), third degree. Class B felony. Plea: Guilty.
2 —NY Penal Law §220.44: Criminal sale of a controlled
substance in or near school grounds. Class B felony. Plea:
Guilty.

*Two years and three months. Wallkill, Ulster, Wood-
bourne, Mohawk, Bare Hill Correctional Facility. Young
man,* the judge says, *let this be a lesson to you.* Gavel
cracks against wood, echoes in the courtroom where we
sit beside our mothers and fathers who are over, *How
could you do this? We gave you everything. Everything!*
As if their immigrating to this Promised Land, the
Land of Opportunity, should've ensured their offspring's

success. We have been summoned home for the week-end. We've emailed bosses at part-time jobs and internships and requested two days off, have cancelled dates with friends and study groups and potential lovers, all of whom know nothing about our lives in the dregs of Queens.

Lying in our childhood beds, we play and replay the scene as we imagine it: Our brothers, our beautiful brothers, deal Dexedrine, Percocet, PCP-laced pot, Ecstasy, Vicodin. Deal at LaGuardia and Nassau community colleges and private schools like Hofstra, Molloy, and NYIT on Long Island. Peddle to students, some of whom are their classmates. Do these people even see our brothers? And do our brothers see them—or are they merely objects to be exploited, a means to an end? We imagine their red-rimmed eyes, how they never want to sleep. Our brothers, blitzed, beside them. *I'll do some construction gigs, save money, then jet.* Blue lights, red lights flashing. The ear-splitting wail of sirens so loud they drown out the music. Our brothers' fingers coiled around doorknobs, so very close to leaving. *Put your hands where we can see them. I repeat, PUT YOUR—* Plainclothes cops lock handcuffs on their wrists. Our brothers, invincible until they are not.

(Icarus with singed wings, falling.)

On our brothers' last night in Queens, we peer into their bedrooms, no bigger than a box. Stretched on floors, we see their lips parted, their eyes cast at ceilings.

But boys don't cry. Boys don't cry. (Boys weep.) Before they leave the next morning and our fathers drive them to Wallkill, Ulster, Woodbourne, Mohawk, Bare Hill, we say goodbye with an embrace. Inhale the tobacco and pine deodorant on their skin. We'll visit you soon, we say. Our mothers struggle to wish them goodbye. They are so angry they cannot bear to face their sons. (Wonder: Is anger inherited?) Instead, our mothers say nothing. Not a word. (Is silence, too?) When our families' minivans round the corner and disappear, our brothers vanish, as well, as if they'd never existed. Only then do we creep into their rooms. Crawl into their beds, which feel like coffins.

TRISH

WE ARE NOT PRESENT ON MARIPOSA AVENUE, A STREET in central L.A. where scraggly palm trees dot sidewalks and loom like scythes against the early-morning sky. We are not present when one woman, a resident who's leaned against her front door at 5:30 A.M. for the last twenty years to smoke her first and only cigarette of the day, is startled by a Mercedes-Benz screeching up the narrow road. We are not present when she sees the car weave then smash into a parked pickup truck, property of her neighbor, two doors down. We don't witness the Mercedes bursting into flames, don't feel the heat that radiates onto the woman's skin, don't smell the scorched rubber and metal, the smoke—chemical, suffocating—that enters the Mission Revival–style houses and disrupts each resident's dreams. Cough, cough. Wheeeeeze. *Wake up!*

No. We are three thousand miles away in New York City. We are in Boston, Philly, D.C., and other East Coast locales. We have not gone far. We are two years out of college—American girls with American degrees. (Never mind that some of us majored in Art and other so-called *impractical fields*—poli-sci, English, international relations, even biology—anything that wasn't a pre-professional track, a clear-cut road to our future selves. *But what,* we're asked on multiple occasions, *are you going to do with that degree, exactly?* When we graduated, our families reasoned, *Well, a degree is a degree!* Subtext: even if those degrees don't put food on the table. Sub-subtext: We are so American we believe our college degrees have nothing to do with skills and salaries. This is our privilege.) Many of us were the first in our families to graduate on American soil. Others of us were the first to earn college degrees, period. All of our parents admonished us to *make something of ourselves.* And we have—haven't we? In this moment, however, we don't have a clue what's happening on Mariposa. We aren't present to witness the residents, clad in pajamas, step from their homes to survey the damage, or hear the sirens wail in the distance and draw nearer.

If it's 5:40 A.M. in California, it's 8:40 A.M. in New York, Boston, Philly, D.C. We grip coffees purchased from cafés that leak from their plastic lids and scald our fists as we rush to work, late again. Some of us are already at offices getting berated virtually and to our faces by our clients and bosses. We think, It's too early for this bullshit. We contemplate making cardboard cutouts of ourselves and plopping them in front of our computers, desks—It's not like anybody would notice. Others of us have stayed up all night to complete our research papers and readings for grad school. We're studying education policy, immigration law, modernist poetry, genome sequencing. We can barely keep our eyes open at labs, libraries, and with our undergrads who prod us awake with their pens. *Professor? Professor!* Many of us daydream about our dates scheduled this evening with the resident doctor, the journalist, the software engineer, the PhD student. We daydream about whether or not we have time to stop by Blink gym or SoulCycle after work. Our minds have already wandered to happy hour. We cannot wait to have a cocktail, a beer—You know what? Make it two—because the day is already shit. (We wouldn't call ourselves functioning alcoholics.) Many of us are still seething from the promotions we didn't receive, our job reports deeming our work "unsatisfactory," the less-than-stellar reviews and comments on our latest gallery exhibits, dance performances, articles.

In short, we are so wrapped up in ourselves.

No, we aren't present on Mariposa Avenue when firefighters arrive to douse the Benz, and three EMTs pull the brown girl from the dented metal—*The only victim, thank goodness!* the residents say. *Jesus Christ, what was she on?* We aren't present during the doctor's official report: *Female, age twenty-four. Cracked frontal lobe, burns covering ninety percent of her body. Dead on arrival. Time of death, 5:47 A.M.*

We are not there to witness the EMTs place a white sheet over her still frame.

(When glimpsed from a bird's-eye view, the white fabric resembles a patch of snow.)

Nor are we present when two NYPD officers at the 106th Precinct in Queens—having received a call from the LAPD—drive to her childhood home. In the kitchen where she'd once eaten meals, her mother prepares a dinner of chicken curry and brown rice. Her father, home early from his shift, watches the 6 P.M. news.

Knock, knock.

Officer?

Please—take a seat.

We are so sorry this happened.

Three days later, after Trish's burial on Long Island—Long Island, a place that's revered by our families for being cleaner, quieter, more spacious, and of course, whiter; in short, all the things Queens will never be—we gather at her childhood home. We have not seen one another in months, years. We stare at a photo of Trish propped on the coffee table in the living room where she did homework and called us on the phone. Photo reveals: her high school graduation, Townsend Harris. The tassel on her cap brushes her temple, threatens to lodge into her left eye. She clasps her hands behind her back and tilts her head ever so slightly to the side—the image of a poised, respectful girl. Obedient, good.

But some of us detect something askew in her gaze.

Watch out, motherfuckers, her smile says.

* * *

Do you remember when? our stories begin and continue for the rest of the evening until we are too tired, too sad, too drunk, too sick of one another, until we remember how much we want to leave and do—Do you remember when she baked me a Funfetti cake for my twelfth birthday, had me pretend to blow out the candles in the lunchroom? Do you remember when she stood up to Vanessa Kleinberg and her clique and told them to go fuck themselves after they called Shay smelly and made her cry? Do you remember when, in high school, she had us dress in Amanda's saris and take the train to Times Square, so she could make a video of us for her film class?

One of us, Rachael, says: In our junior year of college—she was at FIT, and I was at City—she invited me to this festival that her student film was featured in. You know, the one that won the award? I remember she wore this dress with tiny beads embroidered on black mesh. She looked so confident and stylish when she stood onstage and accepted her prize. At the after-party, swear to God, there were so many rich kids. I knew they were loaded by the way they carried themselves. And I wasn't wrong— they told me about their apartments in the Village, their films financed by trust funds. When Trish won, I was so damn proud of her. Halfway through the night, she told me to wait outside this room. To knock if anyone was about to enter. After twenty minutes, I thought, What the hell is taking so long? I opened the door, and there was Trish with four other girls bent with their noses on top of the table. I shut the door, but not before she caught my eye. I left the party. I just didn't want to be there anymore. Trish followed me, kept calling my name. But I ran to the subway before she could reach me. Do you remember when, do you remember when.

That was the last time I saw her.

*   *   *

Goodbye, Mrs. Singh, we call to her mother when we leave. Kiss her cheek.

Girls, she says, thank you for coming. Get home safe.

To one another, we give curt nods. Offer weak smiles and even weaker promises. See you next time, we say, but make no definite plans. We raise our hands and wave goodbye, but when we catch sight of our palms moving like windshield wipers beside our heads, we suddenly feel stupid. When we lean in to embrace one another in the same way we hugged Trish at the lunch table, our embraces are clumsy. Distant. This time, there is no Trish.

We return to our apartments. To dishes in the sink, bathrooms with tubs in need of a scrub, to three, four, five roommates, to lovers who kiss our backs soothingly beneath comforters. We shut our eyes.

When we open them, a voice greets us—Trish's. In our dreams, we are eleven, twelve years old again. Trish is dressed in her middle school gym uniform, polyester pants loose against her slim figure. She leans against an empty bike rack in the school courtyard. Above us, the seagulls circle and screech. The sky is cloudy, the color of pavement. She calls our names once more. We don't take a step toward her. Not yet. We take in the moment. There she is again, our old friend, smiling.

PART FOUR

THOSE WHO LEAVE &
THOSE WHO STAY

S O WHAT'S NEW WITH YOU? IS THE QUESTION WE HOPE our friends who have remained in the dregs of Queens will ask when we visit, but never do. We have moved away from this neighborhood, have been gone for five years since graduating college. But our friends who've stayed anchored to the hood want to spend forty minutes talking about which of our old classmates got knocked up, yet again. I mean, how could you be dumb enough to be a baby mama TWICE? they say. They fill our time with what stupid shows they binge-watched for eight hours on Netflix, what bars, with names like Party Gyal, they squandered their paychecks at, what moldy hookah they smoked on Jamaica Ave. Some of our old friends tediously describe each article of clothing they purchased from Queens Center mall, listing each object's price. In the clearance aisle at Macy's, they say, I found this olive green peacoat for thirty-seven dollars, these Steve Madden boots with cute buckles at the ankles for twenty-nine dollars, a Calvin Klein dress half-off for forty-five, but I think I'm going to return it, and get this *OTHER* dress for blahblahblah. Notice that it is our friends who make the least money who shop the most. We no longer live at home like our friends, who drone about weekends spent at malls and nights occupied by some sad party, and we wonder if these are truly the most interesting events going on in our friends' lives. We notice that none of them bring up their breakups, their layoffs, their families, or anything of importance until we prod them.

So what's new with you? If they *do* ask, they do not *really* want to know. We do not tell them about the latest documentary we're shooting, our promotions to Creative Director, Senior Business Analyst, Head Teacher, we do not mention the research we're doing for our grad thesis in public policy, genome sequencing, Cold War relations. We do not make the same mistake as we did the first time we visited, bringing up the shit we were excited about. Because when we did, we were taken aback by the flash of jealousy in their eyes. When we tell them to visit us in our new neighborhoods in Brooklyn, Manhattan, the trendy parts of Queens, they snort and say, Look at you. Yuppie. So instead, we respond, Nothing's new. Same old. *What, you think you're better than us?* Leave, they say, why would we ever leave?

But those of us who have stayed with our families in Queens, though some of us have moved to our own apartments in the same neighborhood, when our friends who've left visit, we play it cool. We know that these girls don't give two shits about loyalty, wouldn't recognize it if it smacked them, dead on, in their smug, arrogant faces. We know these girls don't give a *damn* about anyone other than themselves or anything, anyone, outside their own stupid orbits. They don't help their mothers pay mortgages, don't give a flying fuck that their dads have lost their jobs and haven't been able to find new ones. They don't buy groceries, they don't drive their grandmothers to physical therapy. They don't remember the sound of their mother's voice after a shift at the hospital when she says, *I'm so tired.* They aren't fazed when we mention our worries at the sight of more MAKE AMERICA GREAT AGAIN signs populating the streets where we grew up. Instead, they stifle a yawn and say, Well. All we can do is move forward. We grind our teeth and glare—when the fuck did they stop caring? They assume, when they visit, that nothing has changed, they wear their designer watches, sigh and check the time, they think we do not notice the pity in their eyes, reserved especially for us, when they return. We try hard not to slap their smiles, so fucking condescending. We must stifle our laughter when they talk—pretend—like they don't come from this neighborhood themselves. As if they were born somewhere else. Our friends who've left simply want to believe that nothing has changed and yet, they've missed Hema's daughter's first steps and were the last to know Rose's mom had a stroke. They don't know Sheila's working two jobs now, that Maryam went back to school after the assault and finished her degree—We're so fucking proud of you, we'd said to her. They didn't come out for drinks to celebrate Ebony passing her board exam or for Kim's going-away party before she left for the Peace Corps. Then again, maybe they weren't even invited in the first place.

No, our friends who've left don't have a clue. They've forgotten these streets. But that's the difference between them and us: We don't forget. We've never become strangers.

HYPER / VISIBLE / IN / VISIBLE

BROWN GIRLS BROWN GIRLS BROWN GIRLS WHO, IN A nutshell, become big shots. Who sit atop stages in London, Sydney, Hong Kong, and in front of lecture halls at Princeton, NYU, and Oxford, who speak on panels and give interviews and lead conferences and are quoted as experts on the state of X,Y, and Z. Who utter sentences that begin *The ways in which* and *The intersection of* and *It's apparent this work is emblematic of* blahblahblahblah. Oh lord! Excuse us, but could somebody please cut out our tongues? We touch the masks we've learned to wear, gaze into mirrors at our "better" selves. Lieberry. Sorry, sorry—Lie-brair-ree. We stutter: Lie-lie-lie-brary. Library. We are congratulated: *What a splendid presentation you gave! An excellent performance!* We mash our fingers to our straining smiles.

Thank you! we chirp. It's so wonderful to be good! It's so wonderful to be good enough.

Afterward, in bathrooms replete with air fresheners that automatically spritz a cucumber-and-cantaloupe perfume at specified intervals, a scent that does not completely mask the underlying smell of piss and shit, we perch on toilets. We grasp the edges of our masks and find we cannot tear them from our faces.

We gain recognition for our work. *How does it feel to have achieved* SO MUCH *as a Woman of Color in your field? What does Your Community think of your work?* (Are you their hero, villain, savior?) *What do you make of the state of* [fill in the blank] *in the U.S. with regard to your art, your research?* Of racism, immigration, the newly elected president, formerly a businessman and reality TV star—Do you know he's from Queens, too? We stiffen. We are determined to keep our responses apolitical, lest we offend. We are afraid to bite the hand that feeds us. Because we are the *good immigrant daughters,* the *oh-so-hard-working ones,* the *paragons of the American Dream,* aren't we? (But for what? For whom?) Nobody asks about the work itself. We are so visible we have become invisible. Odd that in this moment we dreamt of, we are faceless.

ART

OUR SAVIOR, OUR VANQUISHER—NO, VESSEL—OF FUNK! our eighteen-year-old selves once proclaimed.

But, as we age, our twentysomething-year-old selves understand the truth: Our funk is ever-present.

Funk when our words, our choreographies, our sculptures and films and essays fall short of what we envisioned and set out to do. Funk when our work is expected to speak for our so-called "communities," our "cultures." Funk when we feel as if we've been relegated to a box, a cage, or as if we were an indecipherable species meant to be observed beneath a microscope, or from an arm's-length distance. Funk when our work is misunderstood, deemed insufficient—*Not adequately engaging with themes of identity, a bad example for the youth of our community, uninstructive, lacking moral clarity, a poor representation, why did you choose to por-*

tray X in this light?, and *how can you claim to speak for all?* (But, we protest, we never promised any of these things!) (*Too bad. As examples of Your Race, you must surely speak for all!*) Funk when we are told to make ourselves decipherable, palatable, acceptable. (But for whom?—SHHH!)

Funk when we feel we are never, will never, be enough.

These voices drive us to the brink, cause us to compromise, pander, repress, deny. Erase ourselves. In our moments of weakness, when we listen to these voices filled with unspoken expectations, intentionally malicious or just plain ignorant (but, in the end, is there really a difference?), messages explicit or insidious—we come to loathe ourselves. We create objects that merely masquerade as art: hollow entities possessing no truth. We despise the work we've created. We despise ourselves.

Art, our prison.

AMNESIA

WE BURROW DEEPER INTO OUR BEDS WHEN WE HEAR our alarms ring on a morning that feels anonymous, identical to every day that came before. As usual, we shuffle from our beds, brush our teeth, throw on pants, smooth down collars. We make our way through the day, until slowly, glancing around, it dawns on us that everyone we interact with—our coworkers (white), our bosses (white), our neighbors (white), our friends from yoga (white), the families who lounged around us on vacation (white), our ex-lovers (primarily white) and our current ones (white), the baristas (white), our dog-walkers (white), and even our goddamn manicurists (white)—are all white. When did this happen? (Are we, too, w— SHHH! Don't. Say. A. Single. Word!) This realization sends us rushing from our offices and condos on the Upper East Side, in Chelsea, in FiDi, fumbling with the keys to our BMWs and Benzes and Teslas, which, yes, even in this city, some of us can afford. We speed down roads, curse jaywalkers on the streets. Curse ourselves. We drive like madwomen, weaving in and out of traffic. Who the fuck are we? we think. On the radio: the president's voice. The newscasters analyzing the latest poisonous thing he said.

Flying through the streets, we remember an incident from earlier in the week, a memory we'd hoped to repress. During happy hour with our coworkers and bosses, on dates with people we'd met through apps, dinners with our potential in-laws, and even lunches with our own family members whom we hadn't seen in months, the sentence: *He's doing a great job as president, isn't he?* Hearing this, we'd frozen in confusion. Responded by mumbling something vague. But others of us—the ones too entrenched in these new worlds we inhabit, too desperate to be accepted by our coworkers and lovers and in-laws, too ignorant to think for ourselves—chimed in in agreement. (*Marionettes on a stage, spotlights hot and blinding.*) Others of us simply stayed silent. (*Good girls. Don't fuck it up!*)

Some of us, however, upon hearing this, fought against our instinct to scream.

But we don't hold back now.

Our shouts reverberate in our ears, dissipate into the smoggy sky.

On impulse, we speed over the Brooklyn Bridge. We pass the gleaming cobblestone streets and brownstones in Dumbo, Brooklyn Heights—No no no no, we think—and we continue heading south. Eventually, we come upon a roundabout surrounded by leafy trees, and we guess we have reached Midwood? Lefferts Gardens? A procession of people on the avenue forces us to slow down. A wedding celebration. We observe the Hasidic Jewish men's furry spool-shaped hats sitting atop their heads. The families are joyous, chanting. We feel a pang of envy.

We keep speeding south. Note the apartment buildings, the two-story row houses that grow worn and boxy with less attention paid to beauty, and greater concern for tight construction budgets. We spot an increasing number of discount stores: Save-A-Thon, SuperDeal 99¢, and COOKIE'S, whose logo boasts HIGH FASHION, LOWEST PRICES! We drive past a sprawling Jehovah's Witness Hall and Jazzy's Beauty Supply advertising a WIG SALE! EBT signs written in red block letters come into view, along with liquor stores with faded awnings and delis featuring bouquets of flowers in garish shades out front. These sights calm us.

Hit the parkway again. Keep driving until we reach the edge of Brooklyn. Here, in this neighborhood, the overhead subway tracks stretch like a monster's spine. Storefronts crowd the avenue. It's a sight that feels fa-

miliar, except for the fact that many of the signs here,
wherever we are—Brighton Beach, Sheepshead Bay?—
are written in Cyrillic alphabets:

> **Киев Аптека**, which also houses a
> WESTERN UNION, both located
> beneath a psychic's office

Українська католицька церква, beside a
massive Virgin Mary statue, her palms pressed
together, head bent in piety

We drive past Imperial Furs where coats made of
dead foxes adorn mannequins. Next door, Eurasia Nails
features a photo of a ghostly hand photoshopped with a
French manicure. Sights that overcome us with the familiar sensation of the rest of the world now jumbled
onto a single avenue. The McDonald's, Target, Costco,
and Bank of America, however, remind us that we're
still in the U.S. of A.

What journeys, we wonder, did the people who now
live in these neighborhoods take? How did they make a
home?

Who the fuck are we?

Not far from the avenue, the Atlantic Ocean glim-
mers. We pull over. Get out. Breathe in the briny air. For
a second, we are certain we have been beamed to the
dregs of Queens—a place, we realize, we didn't have the

courage to face today. The afternoon is blindingly sunny. We walk along the shore. The wind tangles our hair. Here, amidst these stores and languages, this ocean—we are reminded of the girls we used to be. (*Blue lips puckered for a photo, smile!*) Before our promotions, our raises, our oh-so-tasteful homes, replicas of West Elm displays. Where are our friends now? we wonder. And what happened to the girls we left behind?

HAUNTING

ONCE AGAIN, SHE COMES TO US IN OUR DREAMS.

Her black dress embroidered with delicate beads sways at her knees, and slivers of skin flash from beneath the gauzy material. This time, we are the ones who call to her.

Trish! Trish! we say.

But she turns her back to us, begins to walk away. We follow her impatiently down the sidewalk. Bodies swarm around us and mountains of garbage bags line our path, make it impossible to reach her. Still, even from a distance, we can spot the nape of her neck, the corner of her dress. Why won't she stop?

Wait! we shout.

We have not seen her in years. There is so much we want to tell her.

We do our best to maneuver around the crowds, but

fail. Despite the sea of people, her gait appears unencumbered, serene. We stop pushing forward only when the light around us inexplicably dims. We grow cold, shiver. We strain our eyes to peer into the sky beyond the Chrysler, the Empire State Building, the billboards that line Times Square assuring us that we, too, could buy happiness in the form of the latest iPhone, and Sephora's anti-aging night serum, and American Eagle's high-waisted jeans. Beyond the endless vertical maze of scaffolding, the sun has vanished. But we catch a glint of its rays from behind a cratered moon: an eclipse. We start to sprint in the direction we'd seen Trish go.

We keep calling her name. Trish! TRISH! The crowds of people have disappeared. We run through the empty streets. The concrete morphs beneath our feet into earth blanketed with grass that bends in the wind.

We're on a cliff. The air is so pure, it is painful when it fills our lungs. We stop running when we reach the cliff's edge.

Where has she gone?

Below us, a steep drop. The ocean's waves curl and foam. We step back, dizzy. A strange scent fills the air—the suffocating smell of scorched rubber, plastic, and hair.

We turn around.

Trish stands behind us. We're so close, we could touch the beads draped across her collarbones.

We realize then that the skin on her face is melted. We bite back a scream.

Trish? we say. Is it really you?

Yes, she whispers.

It's been so long.

She says something else we can't understand. We lean closer. What was that?

She tucks a loose strand of hair behind our ears. At her touch, we close our eyes. We feel her palms rest on our shoulders.

I said—wake up.

And then she shoves us. Our heads snap back from the force of her touch. Our arms flail. There is nothing to hold on to as our bodies soar down

down

down

through the open air.

We are falling, falling. Free.

Wake up!

PART FIVE

A TRIP TO THE MOTHERLAND
(FATHERLAND?)

W E TAKE TWO WEEKS OFF, A MONTH, THREE—WE QUIT our jobs altogether. Something pulls us to places we've heard of all our lives, ones that have followed us like ghosts. Beckoned. This time, we do not resist.

We purchase flights to capital cities: Dhaka, Port-au-Prince, Manila, Kingston, and Santo Domingo. In a week, we will fly to Mexico City, Islamabad, Accra, Caracas, Seoul, Damascus, Bogotá. Soon, with our own eyes, we will see San Juan, Cairo, Tehran, Beijing, Panama City, Georgetown, New Delhi, and many more places.

The night after we dreamt of Trish, we woke, covered in sweat, with an urge to call our old friends. We do. We set up dinner reservations at our favorite spots:

an unassuming restaurant in K-Town that serves the best Korean fried chicken, the cozy wine bar on the Lower East Side whose name translates, in English, to "long ago."

It's so good to see you, our friends say. How've you been?

We do not mention our dreams.

These days, we make an effort to see them at least once every few months. When we tell them that we've booked plane tickets to places our families left behind, they screech, You're going back to the motherland?! Well, shit— Watch out for those green card grubbers! No, don't listen to her, bring home someone cute for us! They say, Damn, I wish I could come, too.

For Danica, Amani, Nadira, and Elyse, we remind ourselves to search for lapis lazuli earrings. For Chandra, Rashida, and Melody, handwoven purses. For Rosalee, Nkechi, and Yesenia, billowing pashmina scarves.

When we mention our trips to our families, some of our loved ones are confused. They say, *Why would you want to go back there?* While others are encouraging. *Don't forget to call your second, third, and fourth cousins!* We groan. The most dramatic of us tell our mothers: I'm leaving to find myself! To which our mothers respond, in turn, by scanning us from head to toe.

They say, *But you're already here.*

We'd felt brave boarding airplanes, confident and excited throughout our flights, but when we finally arrive in our ancestral lands, these feelings evaporate. When we set foot in the countries our families always referred to as *home*, we're overcome with the realization that we only know these places in theory: a patchwork of memories, family stories, old photographs, Facebook research on cousins we'd forgotten, news articles, and Hollywood movies where all grit is, in fact, scrubbed clean.

Theory, we discover when we exit airplanes, pales in comparison to the scents, sounds, and feel of these places. Here, we do everything wrong. We pack too many dresses because we assume the temperature will be 100 degrees each day. Instead, when we arrive, rain pours as if from buckets in the sky, soaks through our flimsy dresses, and leaves us shivering. If we *do* remember to pack rain jackets, ones we'd purchased from outlets in SoHo that specialize in "outdoor recreational wear," they fail us, too—because here, being "outdoors" is not "recreational," but the norm. Idiot! When we reach mountain ranges thousands of feet above sea level, places so chilly our teeth chatter, we long for our scarves and gloves and wool hats—items we wouldn't in a million years have thought necessary for our once-in-a-lifetime trips. We curse our families in the States for not warning us—though, perhaps they, too, had forgotten. Our aunts laugh and lend us their own clothing:

oversized coats, caps lined with fleece. For an instant, we resemble them, glimpse alternate realities of lives where we are farmers, shopkeepers, women who bore children young, women who are not strangers to the earth or their own families.

For some of us, when our ancestral lands are, in fact, a sweaty 100 degrees, we don shorts and tank tops. We amble through the streets. When we notice the men and women going about their business dressed in Levi's jeans, ankle-length sundresses, and modest cardigans despite the heat, we feel self-conscious of our naked shoulders and thighs. We forget to use scarves to cover our hair in public and are reminded to conceal our bare legs when we visit temples, mosques, and cathedrals. Loose American women!

American—Is that what we are? we slyly ask our cousins, the ones who tour us around and know these lands in ways we never will.

Yes, because you were born in the States, they tell us. Or, *No, you have Mexican, Filipino, Guyanese, Panamanian, Indian, Haitian, Chinese blood—how could you be anything else?*

We hand street vendors the wrong bills, unfamiliar with the colors of each note. Only when we walk away do we realize we've given ten times the amount we owed, a hundred instead of a ten. Our cousins laugh, say, *You've fed him and his family for a week!* In these countries, we expect palm trees but are met with gleaming skyscrapers. We expect pristine beaches like the photos that populate Instagram feeds and travel blogs and subway ads but discover shores littered with plastic bags and warning signs: POLLUTED WATER, BEACH CLOSED.

What we do not expect: seas of brown people who look like us. Brown people crossing the streets, filling the already overflowing buses, bargaining at outdoor markets, sipping coffees, lighting cigarettes, piling onto motorbikes. What we do not expect: brown hands like our own, which stretch toward us, begging. *One dollar, miss, please one dollar,* children chant in English as they follow us down streets. We expect shacks with aluminum roofs, but do not expect some of our families to call these structures home. Aunties and uncles and cousins invite us inside their abodes, and we smell the faintly mildewed air, see the wooden rooms lacking light because windows are costly to construct. Aunties offer us tea and coffee, cookies, biscuits, stories of our grandparents, and unsolicited advice that makes us smile. We are startled by their generosity and warmth despite, from our perspective, possessing little. When we leave the countryside and head to the cities, we do not expect the cities' glittering wealth to surpass New York's: glassy megamalls, newly constructed trains that sound no louder than a hum when they pull into stations, imposing illuminated bridges that blaze at night.

We're terrified to traverse streets where crosswalk signs are nonexistent. We watch as pedestrians stroll into oncoming traffic. We do not expect the tidal wave of cars and motorbikes and buses to stop for these pedestrians, but they do. We do not expect these pedestrians to survive, but they do. They keep moving. At night, we don't expect the women dressed in miniskirts and stilettos loitering on corners, who share our complexion and hair color and build. Women who could be our sisters, but aren't, who enter cars driven by men who are, more often than not, male tourists—white and two, three times their age. We observe these women's coquettish expressions, their expressions like blank slates.

In the Motherland (Fatherland?), our speech is filled with holes. We don't remember the words for many objects. Some of us flush with embarrassment when we must speak, humiliated by our ineptitude, our jumbled, strangely pronounced words. Some of us must rely on translators, human (our cousins) and nonhuman (apps on our smartphones). *What do you mean you never learned the language?* is a question we are constantly asked. *You're practically mute and deaf here!* Harsh as it is, it's true, and we hang our heads.

A joke:
What do you call someone who speaks many languages?
—Multilingual.

What do you call someone who speaks two languages?
—Bilingual.

What do you call someone who only speaks one?
—American! Ha ha!

But some of us, who have been our parents' translators our entire lives—at parent-teacher conferences, banks, supermarkets—know how to communicate fluently. We discuss politics with our uncles and aunties. They ask questions about the wall the current U.S. president wants to build, and is it true that Muslims are barred from entering the country, and what about the caravan of refugees fleeing gang violence at the border? We discuss all the ways the Land of the Free, under the present administration, currently "welcomes" its newcomers.

All of us have cousins, aunts, uncles, and grandparents who toggle with ease between various dialects and languages, English included. They apologize for their accents, but we don't care—we are in awe of them and could listen to them speak all day.

However, although speech is easy, we learn that the exchange of ideas is not. Our cousins ask, *How much do you earn per month? Do all Americans own guns? Can you really do anything you want when you turn eighteen? Is it true you have sex ed? What do they teach you? What do you mean you don't want to talk about it?* We walk away, exasperated by their endless questions.

Truth be told, though, many of us speak concoctions of ancestral languages and English. Some of us remember words, phrases, even song lyrics, which pop into our heads randomly, as if parts of our brains were being unearthed, or revived.

Still, people do not have to hear us speak ancestral tongues or English to know that we are from another place. Often, we are taller, fleshier, courtesy of the U.S. of A.'s vitamin D–enriched milk, meats, cheeses, and processed foods loaded with sugar and God-knows-what. We wear ripped jeans, have piercings and dyed hair and tattoos inked onto arms, at which our cousins marvel. Some of us, we deduce, are hairier, a byproduct of whatever hormone-injected animals we've consumed. Some of us don't look any different, but are louder, opinionated, and cause rooms to go silent when we share our thoughts. Some of us simply do not cover our mouths when we laugh. We carry ourselves differently.

However, most telling of our American-ness: our shitty stomachs. Our stomachs aren't strong enough for local tap water that is filled with bacteria our sheltered, fragile American guts were never exposed to. Water that could easily kill us. Instead, we drink H_2O that must be filtered and packaged in plastic bottles, or boiled, at the very least.

One evening, for instance, we unwittingly drink

sodas with ice cubes made from tap water. Dumbass! We shit for days. The worst of us are wheeled to clinics, IVs attached to our forearms. Our aunts and uncles shake their heads at our foolishness. So weak, so American.

This is our privilege.

Another night, en route to meeting our cousins—We told them we'd be fine traveling through the city on our own. How hard could it be?—we get lost. We circle the crowded streets and attempt to retrace our steps. Motorbikes and rickshaws zip past our elbows, and we lurch to the side to avoid them. We pass outdoor markets where the scent of meat skewered on sticks barbecuing atop a leaping fire enters our nostrils. We try not to stare at the loads of feet clad in flip-flops, brown toes exposed. Tonight, the humidity is like a sauna and makes us sluggish, tired. Until a downpour of pounding rain, the kind that pummels our arms and heads, is unleashed. We meet our cousins at bars. They hoot at the state of us: our dripping hair, the mascara running down our cheeks, our drenched clothes. *Why didn't you hire a taxi, a tricycle, a rickshaw?!* We give them dark looks and shrug. What do you want to drink? we ask. They keep laughing until we say, SHHH! because we want to listen to the singers croon alongside their guitarists—Though we know duos like these are a dime a dozen in these cities, the live performances and songs sung in languages we only sort of recall still feel new. We wonder if our mothers sat in bars after rainfalls and listened to love songs, too.

Strobe lights flash. Later, a song streams from speakers, familiar because it is—what else?—American. But when we listen closely, hear its chorus split down the middle and multiplied, we realize it isn't the song we know, but a different version. A remix. Still, we sway our hips and shoulders. We start to move, dance. *Hey, Americana!* our cousins shout, tease us. We pirouette, we vogue, we salsa, we moonwalk, we twerk our bottoms, we move like swans. We grin. We can't help it. After all, we're still girls from Queens.

HERITAGE / INHERITANCE

WE VISIT A TOWERING MAUSOLEUM MADE OF MARBLE and sandstone constructed by an emperor for his beloved; we glimpse its mirror image, ethereal and serene, in the reflecting pool. We ascend the steps of temples, adorned with statues of jaguars and serpents, built by astronomers to observe constellations and distant planets, the sun and moon. We walk through the ruins of an ancient city that span for miles, touch the ivy and moss that cover its stone walls, ponder the carvings of apsaras with coy expressions and lithe, dancing arms whose faces we're surprised to encounter in dark corners. We enter soaring cathedrals commissioned by conquistadors, and we genuflect at the altars before statues of Mary and Jesus, who have been placed—we're surprised to see—beside figures of local gods: our favorite is a rascal whose teeth are bared in a growl. Brown girls brown girls brown girls who, of all the sights they've seen, love these unexpected fusions most.

Other unsanctified combinations we adore: baguettes stuffed with sweet minced pork, English Breakfast tea served with dollops of condensed milk that glob to the bottoms of our cups and tastes delightfully, shockingly sweet. But not just food. We take note of the many hospitals and schools named after people whose life missions, they believed, were to *uplift savage nations.* Understand, in a way we hadn't realized before: we are the descendants of these so-called savage people. Colonized, forever changed, but still here. We do not view these sights and tastes and histories as contradictory, inconsistent. Brown girls brown girls brown girls who, in their bones, are beginning to understand that they are the sum of many identities, many histories, at once.

The colonized, the colonizers. Where do we fall?

Here, we're told, is the plaza where revolutionaries were executed via hanging, via firing squad, for attempting to overthrow colonial rule. Here are the mansions and fields that were gifted to those who worked with the ruling class, in exchange for selling out their own people. Here is the white-walled castle, constructed like a fortress, bordering the cerulean sea, and here are its dungeons where men, women, and children were forced into ships that traveled across the Atlantic, then sold as slaves in Britain, France, the Americas, their colonies. Here are the registers where people were forced to change their names to Spanish, English, French, Dutch ones. Santos, Díaz, James, Roberts, Moreau, Laurent, Janssen. Here are the churches where natives were told to convert. Here are the red-light districts that have sprung up beside naval bases—supply and demand, you know. Here are the sweatshops owned by Apple, Nike, Adidas, Gap, and H&M; the crowds of women pouring onto the streets mean they've just finished their twelve-hour shifts. Here are the call centers where, even though Americans get angry because they claim they can't understand the workers' accents, the workers say they're still grateful to make nine dollars an hour—That's a fortune here! And here's the city—yes, this entire city—that was once blown to pieces by bombs. Where even though we walk through its quiet streets now, we still see ghosts.

*   *   *

The colonized, the colonizer. Where do we fall?

*   *   *

Realize: Whether we like it or not, we lay claim to both.

THE THINGS WE CARRY

W E LOAD OUR SUITCASES WITH GIFTS FOR OUR LOVED ones back home. *Home*—New York. And yet, some of us feel a newfound kinship to these lands. We've purchased pastries wrapped in colorful sheets of plastic that make a crinkling noise when opened, peppers the length of our pinky-fingers, which taste most flavorful when added to steaming broth. We've stuffed our luggage with bottles of liquor our fathers couldn't find in the States. At the behest of our cousins who once studied or worked in the U.S., we begrudgingly carry a bag of yams home. *They're richer, yummier!* our cousins claim. We lug these items and more over continents and oceans, past grim-faced TSA officers. When we finally hand them to our loved ones, they say, *I could have gotten this at the market in Jackson Heights!* But when they bite into these snacks, study their gifts, and we register the pleasure that spreads across their faces, we know we've done the right thing.

We carry seashells strung onto threads, decorative pieces for our grandmothers to hang by their bedroom windows. We carry gold fashioned into necklaces that we clasp around our mothers' necks. *Oh darling, you shouldn't have,* our mothers say. We return with garments we'd bargained for in ancestral tongues and English: silk the color of jewels, wool to withstand Northeast winters, skirts printed with dizzying, geometric patterns. In our suitcases we carry leather sandals and cooking knives, carefully wrapped, for our fathers. We carry letters handwritten by relatives who'd asked us to deliver them to family members in the States. *Dear Auntie,* these letters begin, *I graduated summa cum laude this year. Thank you for funding my college education . . .* They read, *As you may already know, my youngest son, your nephew, passed away of dengue fever. If you could please send money for the funeral, we'd be most grateful . . .* They read, *Our elder brother will be undergoing an operation next month. Could you send funds for his surgery and medication? Our Western Union number is . . .* We carry photo albums with yellowing pages, salvaged by aunts. What's this? we'd asked when they handed them to us. We thumb through albums and stop at a picture of a group of friends by a riverbank. *Can you spot your mother?* our aunts asked, and when we look closely, we're startled to recognize her smile, carefree, captured mid-laugh.

We carry these items and more. We carry the tangible and intangible. Tangible: We arrive in New York with our skins burnished darker shades of brown. Intangible: the fact that we couldn't care less about our darker skin. After walking through streets filled with people who look like us, our time away has shifted something within—we are proud of our complexions. Intangible: memories of the humid air from sunrise to sunset, the nights of unceasing rain, the feeling that we have seen mirrors of who we could have been had our families stayed, had they never left, had we been born in lands we may or may not love, lands that are part of us, regardless.

At the end of our trips, however, the outcome is always the same: we leave, we leave, we leave. We always leave.

It's in our blood to leave.

On planes headed back to the U.S. of A., we stare out tiny windows that grow foggy from our breath. Our loved ones' faces flit through our minds—people we'd met for the first time or reconnected with after years, people we had heard many stories about: our parents' siblings, our grandparents, and cousins, whose features we can trace on our own faces.

Aboard airplanes, we're overcome with a strange feeling. A sensation not unlike déjà vu. That we have somehow been here before.

But how could this be?

We leave, we leave, we leave. We always leave. It is in our blood to leave.

But perhaps it's also in our blood to return.

Why did we ever believe home could only be one place? When existing in these bodies means holding many worlds within us.

At last, we see.

PART SIX

MEANWHILE, IN QUEENS

A GOAT AMBLES ONTO THE BOULEVARD OF DEATH IN ST. Albans, a neighborhood where artists, jazz musicians, and athletes like Jackie Robinson, Ella Fitzgerald, Count Basie, and W.E.B. Du Bois once lived. The goat (breed: Boer; color: gray with white splotches) pauses to eat from a patch of grass in front of an apartment complex built the year Kennedy died, 1963. Across the street from the complex: a church proclaiming THE END OF THE WORLD and a deli inviting you to PLAY YOUR LUCKY NUMBERS HERE! The goat has escaped a nearby Trinidadian-owned slaughterhouse, perhaps sensing its fate. (Headlines in the *New York Post* will read, *He's Ba-a-a-d & He Knows It!*) In Ozone Park, a neighborhood five and a half miles from St. Albans, an outdoor market only open on weekends, known simply by the neighborhood's working to middle-class residents as The

Flea*, sprawls across a gigantic empty lot located beside the Aqueduct Racetrack. As girls, we snuck into The Flea, too broke to pay the six-dollar entrance fee, crouched through a torn section of the wire fence. Our movements mirrored that of some vendors who'd crossed the border from Mexico, sometimes hailing from countries farther away: Guatemala, Honduras.

Some of our loved ones had crossed, too. They fled famine, towns run by drug cartels, gang members who knocked on their front doors, said, *Join us, or we'll burn down your business, your house, kill your family.*

We traveled at night, our families said. *My daughters, what choice did we have? Tell us, what future did we have there? And now,* they say, *look at everything we've accomplished. Living our dream.*

But how can a place be a dream? we wonder.

At The Flea, some of us lived for sorting through heaps of used clothing, a treasure trove, in order to discover cashmere, genuine leather, Yves Saint Laurent. Others of us didn't give two fucks about clothes, didn't have the patience. That shit probably belonged to some dead lady, we said. Some of us preferred, instead, to sink our teeth into roti purchased from food trucks beside vendors' cars. Yelped when steaming chunks of chicken burst from the bread and scalded the roofs of our mouths. Some of us simply wandered around the tents.

---

* Also affectionately called "Le Flea" by brown girls.

When we were kids, we did not yet realize The Flea was identical to markets in third world countries—Excuse us! *Developing nations*—from which we could trace our DNA. Markets in countries we'd visit years later, and be reminded of Le Flea, our hometown.

Decades later, the market is shut down, its vendors told to *scram!* so a casino can be built in its place. Buses roll into our old neighborhood and park beneath the thirty-foot blood-red sign that now reads PARADISE CITY. (Red, the color of 3-by-6-inch envelopes gifted to us as kids during Lunar New Year. Red, the color of wedding saris. Or hell—however you choose to see it.)

Meanwhile, a tech company worth billions and named after a rainforest (now rapidly shrinking IRL), a company whose employees reportedly piss into empty bottles for the sake of efficiency, threatens to move into our home borough to build their headquarters. Some residents fear unimaginable rents, Queens' economic metamorphosis into a second San Francisco. Others argue in favor of the twenty-five thousand new jobs, the billions of dollars in revenue for the local economy, and for the chance to let New York become the *true* tech capital of America. (*But we're* already *the second richest city in the U.S.*, some retort. *Why not spread the wealth, you bastards?*) Hush hush! Elected officials make deals behind closed doors. Protests ensue. The multibillion-dollar company skulks away. Meanwhile, on the shores of Rockaway Beach, tatted hipsters lie on the sand, gobble overpriced mahi-mahi tacos, and surf. The board-walk has now been reconstructed following a devastating category 5 superstorm, its planks now smooth and even, no longer jagged or sectioned off with yellow CAUTION tape. On a summer day, we visit Rockaway Beach. Glance at our middle school, still standing. We buy ice cream cones for a whopping eleven dollars from Ample Hills and eat them at the spot where we'd split a box of popsicles as kids. We lean on the rails and observe the skateboarders and bikers, the children who clutch boogie boards, their sunburned parents ambling behind them. Everything mended, like new.

Surprise, surprise, we think, as we chomp up the remaining bits of waffle cones. It only took a massive fucking hurricane for the city to fix this place up.

GHOSTS

ALL EACH OTHER UP—YO, BERET, FAIZA, XIU, ASHANTI, Soraya!—though some of us haven't spoken in months. I'm back home for the weekend—Oh shit, you are, too? Meet me at Vito's—I'm craving a Sicilian slice like CRAZY! Roam together. This is where I chased an ice cream truck for five freaking blocks, says Edel. That bastard wouldn't stop, he thought it was so goddamn funny to see me wave my bills like a maniac and flag him down—fucking Mister Softee. Wait a sec, whispers Josie. That girl across the street? That was my neighbor Mimi—I can't believe she's pregnant. We haven't spoken since we were thirteen. This is the corner where my brother fought this dude from school, says Khadija. He threw his bookbag on the ground, said, *Watch my stuff.* I almost pissed my pants, and all he'd asked me to do was stand there and wait for him. When he started to get pummeled, homie, I couldn't take it—I jumped on the other dude's back. Punched his head. He threw me off. My skull hit the pavement, but my brother pulled me up, and the two of us ran home. My head was throbbing, and he said, *The fuck were you thinking? Are you crazy?* But he was laughing, and I knew he was grateful even though he never said so. I saw him at Wallkill two weeks ago. Lisa confesses, I ran away from my mom on a day like this. Spent the afternoon in that cemetery by the subway. Didn't come home until it was dark. She beat the crap out of me, my mother. The funny thing is, I was sure she didn't even notice I was gone. This is the corner where that car followed me for four blocks. A shadow passes over Jhanvi's, Luciana's, and Renee's faces. I was twelve. The guy had a gold tooth, said, *I have concert tickets, wanna come?* I ignored him, kept walking. Told myself to stay calm so he'd leave, though my heart was beating like crazy. From the corner of my eye, I saw that he kept smiling at me. Until his arm shot out from across the passenger's seat, and he grabbed my wrist. I dug my nails into his skin, clawed at him. Twisted away. At this intersection, says Dee, I saw a girl get run over by a bus. A high school student. I'll never forget how her body twitched under the bus's fender like a dying bug. I threw up on the sidewalk. Cried all the way home.

THE LUCKY ONES

OUR BROTHERS, OUR BROTHERS WHO GROW UP, TOO. Who do not like to speak of their pasts. *I'm a different person now.* From the corners of our eyes, we watch them kneel on prayer mats three times a day, limbs poised toward the sun. We watch them walk to churches down the block, crisp Bibles nestled in back pockets, we wave goodbye as they drive to temples in Flushing, Richmond Hill, where they enter rooms filled with candles and the murmur of chants like voices underwater. What, we wonder, do our brothers confess to their gods? What secrets do they reveal, what sins? Light a joint when they return. Let the smoke pool in the air, pour them a splash of whiskey. *Thanks, sis*, they say. *Just what I needed.* But some of our brothers only swirl their glasses. Do not take a sip. *Johnnie Walker—just like our uncles!* they laugh, and we relish the sound of it. Until, beneath their laughter, we register something tight. Wounded. Our brothers say, *You know, this was what I was drinking right before the cops came?* We freeze, too afraid to hear the rest. We never did ask the details of that fateful evening, or their time away. Instead, we busy our hands, begin to scrub the stoves in our kitchens. Our brothers continue, *I haven't touched a drop since.* But some of us, after hearing their stories, wind our fists back, and hurl our glasses at walls. In doing so, our helplessness and rage find a fraction of release. When we hear the shocking sound of glass bursting, shattering at our feet, prickling our arms and toes, we welcome the sensation. *Chill!* our brothers shout.

Some of us, when we do hear their stories, fall silent. We can't meet their eyes, which remind us of our mothers' eyes, our grandmothers' eyes. *Don't cry,* our brothers tell us. *You don't have to cry.*

Our brothers break our hearts over and over again. When they cannot find work because of their records, they slink back to their old ways. They do not tell us, but we know.

Some of our brothers simply vanish, and every day we wait for an email, a text. Months pass. One day, they appear on our doorsteps. Hands stuffed in jacket pockets, their hair shaggy. We thought you were dead, we say through clenched teeth. *Dead? Come on, sis*—and here, they call us by our names: Cristina, Jade, Divya,

Zainab, Kelly, Caitlin, and our nicknames, too—*You were always so dramatic.* Shut the fuck up, we say.

We let them in. We always do.

Our brothers are difficult to love. We loan them 5K and they do not repay us, we lend them our cars for a day, which they crash on the Boulevard of Death, we sign to be guarantors for apartments and they fuck us over, leave us with half a year of rent to pay. We tell our friends, That fucking bastard, I *hate* him. We do not speak to our brothers for years, if ever.

We love them and we don't, we love them and we don't—but can you ever choose who you love?

Together, we wash down IPAs at newly opened breweries in Astoria (*Why is this bougie shit so bitter?* our brothers say, their faces puckered). In Bushwick, we etch tattoos (not matching) onto our wrists, rib cages, and thighs—a bouquet of flowers, a robot, names and dates. Our brothers introduce us to their new girlfriends. How long will this one stick around? we think, but we keep our big-ass mouths shut. A few of these women do, stick around. In time, our brothers become husbands, fathers. We, in turn, become aunts. Our brothers cradle their children. *It's like everything was spinning, but she grounds me.*

Some of our brothers make good on their promises from when we were young and sat beside them on basketball courts. They move west. *Not a building in sight, you'd never believe it.* They tell us on phone calls, *I hiked through Yellowstone, the Rocky Mountains, up to God's Thumb, and the Sandia peaks. It's so quiet at night—for once, I can hear myself think.* They laugh. Our brothers who were so silent before. Now, when we visit them in person, they greet us with words that rush like streams past broken dams. Where did all these words come from? We listen to their plans, their dreams and regrets. Our brothers, silent no more.

You asshole, we tell them each time. Every time. You're so goddamn lucky to be alive.

PATRIOTIC

BROWN GIRLS BROWN GIRLS BROWN GIRLS, INCLUDING, but not limited to: Ruth, Tasnim, Glory, Beatriz, Constanza. Also, Irene, Salome, Fabiana, Helen, and Priya. Not to mention Ashley, Kendra, Nadine, and Zhang, who ask, Why should I bring a child into this world? Who view the earth as a dying mother, a spring devoid of water, where beneath her muddy banks, the drip drip of oil is waiting to be fracked. Like patriotic Americans, we consume gallons of gasoline annually, never mind that these resources gestated for millions of years and will never regenerate in our lifetimes. Already, men scheme for new lands beyond our planet, surfaces and moons to mine and profit from, to colonize and populate without a single glance at the place they've left burning. Earth, an abandoned mother.

Why bring kids into this world, we think, when this shithole would be their inheritance?

Make no mistake, some of us wholeheartedly believe this manifesto. But others, deep down, for all our high-minded talk and ethics and self-congratulatory "self-lessness," these words merely mask our fear of becoming parents. Why can't we say this outright? Some of us shudder to envision all the ways we could fuck up our children. Others of us think of how children would, with-out a doubt, inevitably engulf us, force our lives to be subservient to theirs.

Some of us do not want kids, period. We like our lives just the way they are. We're happy and lack for nothing with our partners; we are single and have no regrets. We are free. Still, we cannot bring ourselves to tell our families our decision. *Maya, Julie Fei, Ligaya— what you're saying is unnatural, unwomanly! Are you that selfish?* Because isn't childbirth what we've all been taught to aspire to? *Raise a family in the image of yourself—oops, God. Your life will change completely when you have kids. You will never know true love until you become a parent.* Or so we've been told.

Patriotic, dutiful girls.

Some of us, however—Kylie, Parveen, Leilani, Josefina—cannot say for sure that we don't want kids. We read books that we hide in our laps in public (*What to Expect When You're Expecting*—This shit is so dated, we think), we watch documentaries (National Geographic's *In the Womb*) and observe cells undergoing meiosis at triple-speed, which makes us even more queasy. Or we avoid research altogether and try not to stare at the woman swaying her child to sleep on the subway. We wonder how it would feel to hold our children in our arms.

Others of us—Simone, Chinwe, Shivani, Angela— think: What about adoption, all the kids who need a home? What about the fact that we don't find sex pleasurable and never have? Or that we don't have partners to have sex with, and wouldn't even want that life if we did? What about in vitro, a sperm bank, a surrogate? We research for months.

Others of us take a good, hard look at our meager savings accounts and rented studio apartments. Continue to read articles about Earth's imminent destruction. Wildfires. Oceans polluted by toxic sludge and industrial waste. The extinction of numerous species. Threats of nuclear warfare. Shitty leaders who place their own interests over people. Why in God's name would it be right to bring a child into this world?

We don't know for sure. But what we *do* know is that to admit our uncertainty would leave us vulnerable, as women, to others telling us how to live our lives.

I'm not ready, some of us think. But will we ever be?

PART SEVEN

SHADOWS

OUR WHITE BOYS, OUR WHITE BOYS WHO ARE NOW OUR husbands and claim us at midnight when the moon is half-hidden. Who curl their fingers over our breasts and thighs and say our names. *Cassandra, Kehlani, Rhea, Jihyun, Tabitha, Shazia, Beth.* More, we beg. Harder. You are everything. We slide our hands down backs damp with sweat. No one can say we do not love our husbands because we do. We are good wives. Close your eyes, our husbands say. We do. We obey. Feel their lips on our necks, stomachs, hips, between our legs. But when we close our eyes, what comes to mind is not our husbands' faces. But his face. Brown boys, the ones we knew and left behind. Faces etched into our minds. Panic—Open your eyes, hurry! Good wives. We are good wives.

Walking past a construction site on a gray day in

Chelsea, we run into them—It's been ten, fifteen, twenty years. We stop, startled. Omar! we call. Julian, Rohan, Anthony, Darius! *Is that you?* brown boy, now grown and dressed in a neon vest, asks. We blush at the sight of his mouth, which reminds us of old teenage desire, naked and unabashed, for him. Lower East Side. We meet our friends for happy hour, hand a twenty-dollar bill to the bartender, double-take when he quips, *Still whiskey and Coke after all these years?* We peer at him, recognize the brown boy we wrapped our arms around in basements in Richmond Hill, Jamaica, Woodhaven, Elmhurst. While Aaliyah crooned, *'Cause I really need somebody. Tell me, are you that somebody?* Holy shit, we say. How are you? For the whole night, we cannot take our eyes off him. Write our numbers on napkins. Leave, trembling. We stumble upon brown boy's murals at a park in Inwood, his sculptures in Astoria. We catch sight of him walking down Wall Street in a crisp navy suit, ordering sushi in SoHo. We swear we must be dreaming. We try not to stare at them and their women, fair- and dark-skinned, who link arms with brown boys, who brown boys hold umbrellas for and kiss on concrete sidewalks.

We travel to New Orleans for our friends' weddings. Tess is getting hitched (finally!) to her long-time boyfriend, Samar. They met while cooking together every night in the shared kitchen of their college dorm at SUNY Albany. Faiza is saying *I do* to Max, a marine biologist, after rejecting her mother's choice for a fiancé. (She'll get over it, Faiza shrugs. I hope). Aurora is marrying their partner, Peter, on Tulane's grounds, where they met. We blow bubbles as the newlyweds parade past us, toss daisies, and wave sparklers that crackle and illuminate the darkening evening.

After, at a jazz bar named Court of Two Sisters, where the party has migrated, we meet a man playing drums. Drums that sound like a match going out, hissing, building to a crash. Reverberating in the dim room. Louisiana accent like caramel against our New York mile-a-minute. He slows us down. Reckless, reckless women. *What's your name?* he asks. We reveal our names, or we do not. Desire, when he turns out the light. When we return to homes in Manhattan, Brooklyn, the dregs of Queens, and beyond, we dream of him and that night forever. Or we flee our husbands. Leave for that brown boy, now grown. Open your eyes, hurry.

JENNY

WE LIE IN BEDS AND OUR MINDS DRIFT, INEVITABLY, TO HER. At temples, we light sticks of incense for every letter of her name, trace her profile, as we recall it, on mandalas printed on mosque carpets and weathered, graffitied church pews. We will spend many years not wanting to want. We can't, we tell ourselves. It wouldn't be right. But after broader, heavier bodies hurt us, repel us, we allow ourselves this pleasure. He puts his hands on me, and I was black-and-blue for days, we whisper to one another on the phone. Never, never again.

Or there are no bruises, ever— We realize we were destined to love women from the moment we first clutch Barbies.

We marvel at our lover's soft body and voice, but aren't fooled—we know the strength within. *You are no daughter to me,* some of our parents tell us. *You only bring shame.* For years, if ever, we do not speak to our parents, nor visit our childhood homes in the dregs of Queens. *I wanted grandchildren,* our mothers say on the phone. We hear the accusation, the longing in their voices, and we hang up, our hearts pounding.

Some of us do. Have kids. We say, My daughter has my wife's eyes.

Some of us marry women, yet never feel quite right. I loved Sarah, Lan, Ijeoma, Jazeera, but. We flee. We remarry men. We remarry women. We remarry nobody.

We do not know how these things happen.

Others of us knew we were girls before anyone else. Some of us were girls in former lives, but would eventually choose not to become women. A few of us aren't sure *what* we are. Some of us will never be sure.

Whatever existences we've lived in the eyes of the world, we re-examine the identities handed to us from even before our mothers pushed us from their wombs. Labels—male, female—we shed, in time.

All of us, instead, learn to make our own worlds. We have come to comprehend that we inhabit many worlds at once.

Yes, some of us learn to undo our shame, the ways we have been bred, trained. Some of us even fall headfirst into love. Our partners, we believe, are stronger than us. We delight in their midwestern ways. Their forest green eyes, their eyes dark as night, their curly hair we twirl around our fingers in bed. Some of us fall in love with other brown girls, kiss them when we visit the dregs of Queens one winter break, kiss them in front of our favorite Thai restaurant in Jackson Heights, kiss them inside the belly of a sculpture shaped like a slanted diamond in Astoria.

I thought about this moment for so long, we confess. We never let go, until we do.

BROWN & BROWN MEANS

LEAVE FOR THAT BROWN BOY, BROWN GIRL, BROWN other, now grown. Open your eyes, hurry!

We step quickly and board subways that lurch forward and cause us to lose our footing. Enter bars. Wait for them. One vodka and ginger ale, one Riesling, one gin and tonic, one dirty martini, we say. Can you make it a double?

Is the desire we feel palpable, marked clear as day on our faces?

Some of us, however, do not tremble. We are calm. We are the ones who've arrived with no makeup, no creams and pastes to conceal our skin, the wrinkles forming by our mouths and eyes. We are twenty-four, twenty-nine, thirty-two, thirty-five, forty-one, but sixteen at heart. We've left our lips unvarnished. Let them see it all, we think. We are not here to impress.

They arrive. How did we forget how beautiful they are? We do our best to memorize their movements, the way they gaze at us, the sound of their laughter. We loved them when we were young—some of us realize our feelings have never faded. We drink them in. Burn them into our memories; we might not see them again after tonight.

Reckless, reckless women!

Don't you know better?

We talk for hours. Brown and brown means, I guess I don't have to explain any of this to you, do I? Means, unlike the white people we've dated and even loved, we do not have to spell out instances where we've been singled out, made to feel invisible, or held as examples of our race. Around them, we do not have to describe the existence of racism in education, policing, healthcare, criminal justice systems. Do not have to spell out white privilege, white supremacy—history, for that matter. We don't have to say: Just because you haven't experienced it, doesn't mean it doesn't exist. When we are with them, it all goes without saying.

Brown and brown means, Do you remember that teacher who threw her shoe at a kid on his way to the principal's office? Man, she was nuts—and whatever happened to him? Means, Tell us what it was like when you moved to L.A., Miami, Chicago, Pennsylvania, North Carolina, Iowa. Means suddenly recalling warnings. *It's not that we're racist, it's just—we don't want you dating* those *kinds of boys. Don't you want better for yourself?* Means wondering if we could love them, for we have seen no models growing up, of a love like ours. *You only bring shame.*

For some of us, brown and brown means unease—after leaving the dregs of Queens far behind, we are no longer used to people whose backgrounds mirror our own.

For others of us, brown and brown means zero understanding, contrary to what we'd hoped or expected. You voted for WHO? we say, disgusted—for we are no longer the silent, desperate girls we used to be. (*Charming! Your friend is so charming.*)

Means realizing that, despite our similarities and shared experiences, we now exist on different planets.

The truth? It does not matter if we meet them for one month, ten years, or once, and only once, that night. Whether we take their hands at the bar, walk through the city together that night, make love after, or abruptly leave, full of regret.

Already, we have been changed.

A RECKONING

WHEN WE RETURN HOME, OUR PARTNERS, THE ONES who are white—Matthew, Joshua, Christopher, Ethan, Connor, Olivia, Taylor, Megan, Chelsea, Brooke, and others—say, *I thought you picked me because you loved me—not because of the color of my skin.*

We turn away; we cannot face them. We don't know what to do with the woundedness in their voices. (Are we more elitist than we'd ever admit, we wonder, to have picked white over brown? —*Coconut! Bitch!*)

Our white boys, our white girls, our white others, who are no longer boys or girls, but our husbands and wives, our partners. Who make us tea and coffee in the mornings, who raise our children, and drive our parents to the doctor's and wait patiently with them at their appointments while we're at work. *Your mom was so stubborn with the nurse—just like you!* they laugh. Changing into worn pajamas at night, we glance at them lying asleep, exhausted from work, cooking dinner, putting our kids to bed. We study them as they fade into dreams. Are their dreams peaceful? (Do they dream of us?) Lying beside them, their words repeat in our heads: *Aren't we together because we love each other?*

We *do* love you, we'd answered.

Yet, how to account for instances like Exhibit A) Our partners' company holiday parties. We are one of three people of color in the room. Their bosses hand us their soiled plates, mistake us for waiters. When coworkers point out their bosses' mistakes (our partners are in bathrooms, unaware), their bosses rush back to us, say, *I'm sorry, Michaela, I didn't have my glasses on!* Our partners fume when we tell them on subway rides home. But their anger and indignation will feel merely comical to us.

We have always felt rage.

Another instance: Exhibit B) We are invited on vacations with our partners' families. At the end of our stays, as we depart beach houses and cottages, head back to our usual lives, the host, who's come to bid everyone goodbye, rushes toward us. *Wait—Halima!* she calls. We turn around. She thrusts a small paper bag into our hands. *I think these belong to you?* she says, an expectant look on her face. Inside, we see crumpled lingerie bottoms. Gaudy, cheap. It takes us a second: Of all the women here, we realize, the host believes these forgotten underwear belong to *us*. They don't—we tell her so, coldly. Though we have done nothing wrong, why do we feel shame? And how to explain this shame? (When we learn the soiled lingerie belongs to our partners' mothers, we do our best not to gag.)

Let's not forget Exhibit C) The subtle flash of shock on our partners' aunts and uncles faces when we are first introduced to them. We are not who they expected. *Could you stand over there for the photo, Gabby?* one aunt says to us, and points to the corner of the room. *In case I need to cut you out later.*

How to explain these experiences? The sum of these everyday humiliations, their accumulative weight?

We've made promises to ourselves to see our old friends more this year, but when we speak of these moments to each other, some of us find that we struggle—not with the right words to describe these happenings—but to articulate our choice to be with the ones we love, the people we've built our lives with.

They don't come from the same background, we concede. They move through the world in completely different ways. But they listen, we say. They ask questions. They don't deny our history, or their privilege. They don't give us their pity or guilt, or force us to absolve them. And that means everything.

Some of our friends understand, tell us similar stories of degradation—a collateral price many of us must seemingly pay in these relationships—and of love for their partners, too. It's complicated, we agree. But some of our friends don't understand; instead, they imply that we are self-hating for choosing white partners, that they themselves are better for picking brown.

But is anything ever that simple?

Many of us are merely women who have tumbled into love. Who must learn to balance history with the individuals standing before us. The ones who have seized our hearts, for better or worse. Who we amble through supermarket aisles with and decide which coffee beans to buy. Together, we walk the Brooklyn Bridge, watch movies at IFC, spend weekend days soaking up the sun in Montauk. Partners who open doors to our homes and greet us with a kiss.

There you are, they say. *What took so long?*

INTERLUDE

WE SEARCH FOR THE UNNAMABLE. WE RUMMAGE through coat pockets—I found it, I think I found it!—but happen, instead, upon faded grocery receipts, hardened, scrunched-up tissues from winter of last year, a tube of lipstick. Shade: Electric Blue. Damn, that's where that went? Curious, we swipe it on once more. We study our reflections and feel futuristic. We pucker our lips, muse, Do I look like Rihanna? In coat pockets, our fingers graze a smooth, circular object. We hold it in our hands—a stone we'd plucked from the ground at Prospect Park. We'd meant to use it as a paperweight until we'd forgotten. We search for the unnamable between the knots of our lovers' spines. Covertly, our fingers probe these secret dips while our lovers wash dishes, push wire carts to laundromats, lie drifting off to sleep on their stomachs. *What are you doing?* our lovers murmur. *That tickles.* We knock back shots of Jameson and Patrón at nightclubs thrumming in Hell's Kitchen and the Lower East Side, where Whitney, ageless, pours through the speakers, *Ohhhhhh, I wanna dance with somebody!* We love when Biggie plays, and Jay, too. We sing along, without shame. When Nicki, 50, and Snoop drop, we know all the lyrics—a fact we'd usually be embarrassed to admit, but now, we don't give a damn. *I ain't sayin' she a gold digger,* we rhyme along with Kanye. When Beyoncé and Cardi play, we sing them, too, with gusto, especially "Bodak Yellow": *I don't dance now, I make MONEY moves.* If we've made it farther than New York, we dance and drink at bars in Berlin, Paris, Bangkok, Cartagena, Lagos. Brown girls brown girls brown girls. Now women. We are twenty-two, thirty-three, thirty-six, nineteen—we stop counting. We are never too young or too old to dance. At clubs, we toss back our heads, laughing, throats exposed and speckled with glitter and sweat. As Rihanna croons, *I'll take care of you,* to Drake, and us. But when we glance at the bottoms of our empty glasses, we find no answers there. Only the leftover scent of vanilla and gasoline. If we are parents—as some of us now are—we search for the unnamable, answers to questions we do not know how to phrase, in our babies' cribs. We adjust sleep sacks swaddling creatures we'd incubated in our bodies. Creatures who now have the shape, feel, and scent of a loaf of sourdough bread. They gurgle and beam at us. Children

who, years from now, although we don't yet know it—
when our babies are no longer babies, when they've
grown taller than us and just as wild—will drag tat-
tered suitcases down staircases. Scream, *I'M LEAVING!*
And we, in turn, will shout, GOOD—GET OUT! But as
soon as these words fly from our mouths, we will wish
we could take them back.

REUNION

FOR AN INSTANT, WE DO NOT RECOGNIZE ONE ANOTHER.
We meet our childhood friends—Celine, Xuan,
Devina, Genesis, Annika, Kathleen, Maria, Salma—at
restaurants on Canal Street, in K-Town, Woodside, Harlem. We travel on subways to see each other, journeys
that felt like nothing when we were in high school, but
are a pain in the ass now that we're older and tired from
work and just want to sleep. When we reach restaurants
and our friends slip in, greet us, we wonder, When did
Angie change her hair? When did Grace lose weight?
We say, Let me see that jacket you're wearing, Jaz! and
grab our friend's hand and twirl her around—Okay,
Miss Fancy! But more striking than these physical
changes are our observations about the different ways
our friends now carry themselves—Was Carla always so

quiet, so shy? Was Huda always so opinionated, and did Luz talk about herself that much before? Did Esme always look so beat, as if she'd run a marathon and back, as if she'd fallen asleep and woken each morning with a weight around her neck? Did Chioma's voice always quiver that way? Did she avert her eyes like that, too timid to make eye contact? Did Marjani always throw her head back when she laughed, uninhibited and not at all like the self-conscious girl we remember? Did Nancy always drink so much, one cocktail after the other, as if the alcohol were water? Was Ruchi's laugh always so nervous? Did Sam sleep around that much? Does Shanice know we already heard about their breakup? If we don't know, and they tell us, is it wrong that we're not surprised because we sensed that person never loved them, that they were too good for them? Is it wrong that we don't recognize Zion, at first, because their voice is lower than it was? Why does it even matter?

We love our friends, still.

Wonder how we, too, have changed in their eyes.

Did our friends always seem so fragile?

We've become strangers to each other, but don't want to admit it. The years have altered us into different women, far from the girls we once were—girls who gossiped at lunch tables, roamed Queens Center mall, swapped mixtapes, and believed we'd never grow apart.

But now? *It's been so long,* we write in texts to one

another. *I'm free this Friday evening . . . Want to grab dinner?* We'd felt foolish asking, wondered if we were chasing ghosts.

What is friendship? we think. A fossil, an old photograph, a puzzle?

We cannot say.

The night drags on, disappears. In candlelit pubs on Atlantic Avenue, barbecue joints by 125th where we wipe the glaze from our fingers, and East Village dives where we catch our reflections in grimy mirrors, we speak only of surface things that don't matter. How did we become this way? When did we stop being the people we needed for each other?

After dinner and two rounds of drinks, because we do not want to leave them yet, we ask our friends to sit beside us on park benches with chipping paint, on couches in wine bars where bottles of Sancerre open with a *pop!* Others of us, when we leave restaurants together, hear music playing. With one look at our old friends, we decide to follow the sound, which leads us into Central Park. We stumble upon an outdoor concert: cellos, violins, a harp play in symphony. We sit crosslegged on the ground, slip off our shoes, let the grass prickle our toes. Grasp for hints of the girls we once were. Even if we cannot fill the silence between us with words, maybe the music will be enough.

If we do manage to speak of our lives, we do so halt-ingly. We are stiff, awkward. How to bridge the years? How to overcome this distance we feel? Some of us are afraid to reveal the events that are happening in our private lives, unsure if we can be vulnerable in the way we once were with one another.

Some of us, however, crack open doors and let our old friends through. We confess, I haven't told anyone, but I fell for another man this summer. We say, She kissed me after work, and then we went back to her place. Is it weird that I didn't feel anything when we slept together? Our confessions bring relief mingled with pain and shame. I let myself forget Brendan, Manny, Selena, Audrey, Hamdan, Taylor, waiting at home. When I got back, they'd already put the kids to bed. *Alma, Atreyi, Justine, Saira, Yun-Hee, Natalie, where have you been?* they said. We confess things we do not want to say out loud, feelings we don't even realize we'd buried. I swear to God, it was just a speck on the ultra-sound. It was nothing; that's what I'd told myself. But why do I keep dreaming of it? We say, My brother? I haven't seen him in months. I hate visiting him there. I can't stand the look in his eyes. We confess, Some days I just want to leave everything behind.

Do you ever feel that way, too?

OUR NOT-REFLECTIONS

W HEN YOU GROW UP, YOU'LL SEE, OUR MOTHERS SAID.
As if, one day, we would suddenly understand why they were the way they were in our girlhoods: overly critical, casually cruel, lacking imagination, close-minded. Afraid. We vowed, then, never to become them. For months, which solidify into years, we do not call much. And when we do, we tell our mothers only what they want to hear, what we believe they can handle: Yes, work is going well. Yes, the children are great. Because to explain the truth of our lives—we've left our partners, we've decided to adopt, we've chosen to forgo children altogether, we are deeply unhappy—or happier than we've ever been—would mean, we think, our mothers forcing us to live another way.

Brown girls brown girls brown girls.

Who age and wonder, is it time that mellows us and

our feelings toward our mothers? That make our memories of them less painful?

Come visit, our mothers say on the phone.

You'll see, they once said, and, in fact, we do, caught in the cycle of our jobs (we are ICU nurses, computer programmers, high school history teachers, art professors, opera singers, bartenders, social workers, accountants), bills that never seem to cease (home, car, fire, life insurance, gas, electricity, water, mortgage, property tax, rent, childcare), and our lovers and children who demand every inch of us (*Can I get a pair of Doc Martens, Mom?* What do I look like, we snap, an ATM?!), until we feel depleted.

We age and soften. At night, we glance into bathroom mirrors. Touch our fingers to our downturned mouths, the pouches beneath our eyes. But, instead of our own reflections, we are startled to see our mothers glancing back at us. We turn our heads to one side, the other. They follow our gaze.

Lying in beds where we cannot sleep, we wonder who our mothers once were—before they were anyone's wife, anyone's mother, grandmother.

We close our eyes.

When we open them, we see our mothers boarding airplanes branded Delta, American Airlines. They are leaving behind former selves in countries we will never fully understand. Our mothers' sights are set on the U.S. of A. The Land of Opportunity. *Goodbye! Goodbye!*

they call to their mothers and fathers, their siblings and friends. We hear the triumph, pride, and anticipation in their voices. *I'm leaving this place!* seated one row behind them, we slouch behind magazines.

We are ghosts from the future.

When they land in New York City, circa 1990, they are greeted by a dizzying array of people with all different skin colors speaking various languages that sound like music. They stroll past trash bags piled high on sidewalks, and graffitied everything—storefronts, cars, alleyways, brick buildings. But they aren't fazed. Their excitement and hopefulness outweigh their fears. They're dying to see the Statue of Liberty, especially Ellis Island, where they heard immigrants like them—people who hailed from countries like Ireland, Italy, Russia, Poland, and many other lands—once passed through. How they journeyed on ships to reach American shores.

We join them on days off from work as they board subways and buses to explore their new home—Can they call it that? they wonder—for the first time. They tour the coast guard's houses on Governors Island, peruse the towering dinosaur bones at the Museum of Natural History, watch the carefree Americans ice skate in Central Park (our mothers' budgets are tight, they can't splurge on tickets themselves), and gingerly perch atop towels at Rockaway Beach where they try not to gawk at women dressed in bikinis. When our mothers are homesick, they discover their favorite foods in a neighborhood not far from them in Queens, called Jackson Heights. They are utterly relieved to find familiar foods, not to mention another place that teems with immigrants like them, that they nearly cry.

When our mothers visit American supermarkets for the first time, we watch as they marvel at aisles of gleaming food, seemingly magical in their limitlessness. *Pineapples all year round?!* (Because what is more American than excess, than not being subject to—than being above—the laws of nature, the changing seasons?) We join them when they plant their feet on snow for the first time and wish their friends were here to see it, too.

Some of our mothers have not met our fathers yet, so we join them on blind dates set up by their friends from work. Some of our mothers have arrived as married women, but must wait two, three, five years before our fathers' visas are processed. During these years, our fathers are but voices on long-distance phone calls. *We miss you,* our mothers whisper into pay phones. A distance we will never know. We stand beside our mothers, who technically aren't yet our mothers, as they sift through racks at Goodwill. We nudge a knee-length eggplant-colored coat we think they'd like in their direction. But they brush past it in favor of a jacket with colorful patches sewn together to resemble a rainbow. We raise our eyebrows in surprise. We study them as they slip on the jacket, admire their reflections. Splurge for $24.99. We sit cross-legged atop toilet seats as our mothers carefully handwash the coat at home in bath-tubs. We fall asleep and wake beside them in apartments they share with four other women. When they rise, we are startled to feel their ambition and excitement, paired with equal amounts of homesickness and loneliness that radiates from their bodies.

Our weary mothers, so practical and unimaginative—or so we believed. Who we were certain never had dreams.

How wrong we were.

But how could *We wanted to make a better life for ourselves—and you*—be a dream? How could a place be a dream? (Did we live up to their dreams? we wonder, uneasy.) Understand that we will never fully comprehend their dreams having come of age in this Promised Land.

Understand: We are their Promised Land.

Never in a million years would we have the courage to move to a foreign country on a dream, become fluent in a strange language, raise families on foreign soil, far from those we love. Raise children who often feel like reflections in foggy mirrors. Who, from the moment they learn to walk, are running farther than they can see.

Resilient, strong, determined, our mothers carved out homes of their own.

This, too, is in our blood.

In the middle of the night, when everything is quiet at last, we pick up phones.

We do not think they will answer at this time. We are surprised when they do.

How are you, Ma? we ask.

We hear surprise in our mothers' voices, recognize an eagerness that mirrors our own.

Oh! they say. *It's you.*

FUTURE TENSE QUEENS

WE HEAD TO THE OPENING OF A PHOTOGRAPHY EX-
hibit in an area of Queens that conjures, in
our minds, miles of empty factories. But when we exit
the subway, we find that we are mistaken, that the images in our minds are outdated. Instead, half a dozen
sleek glass condos under construction, a giant glass
spaceship of a tech store whose logo, portentously, is a
bitten fruit denoting mankind's fall from grace, and a
multinational supermarket catering exclusively to the
first world's oh-so-delicate digestive tracts greet us. We
read the advertisements that line the supermarket's
windows: GLUTENFREEDAIRYFREEKETOPALEOOR-
GANIC. Might as well say bland as fuck, we think. Not
to mention a pain in the ass. We wonder what it must be
like for these glutenfreedairyfreeketopaleoorganic people to travel to countries where meals are cooked in

street markets and woks and charcoal grills in front of them, or sold from the back seat of motorbikes, and little windows from some grandma's tienda or sari-sari. We imagine that, in the (un)likelihood of said people traveling to these countries (*But is it dangerous???*), they sit in restaurants and ask waiters in loud voices, *IS. THERE. ANY. DAIRY. OR. GLUTEN. IN. THIS?* betraying their belief that non-native English speakers must be deaf. We imagine dishes placed before them, and first-world travelers scrunching up their noses, whining, *I can't eat this!* Well, we say, with a smile, we hope you starve. We pass another supermarket, one exported from sunny Californ-I-A. If Hipster Joes is here then, shit, we think, it's all over. (Still, we purchase TJ's frozen spinach pies, their almond vanilla granola, which, in our opinion, taste bomb). Disoriented, we walk through this face-lifted, future tense Queens, all wide streets and waterfront and gantries—whatever the fuck those are. Catch sight of brown faces here and there swimming in a sea of white. Transplants, we surmise, who have escaped the 'burbs for this stroller-laden, newly glossy part of Queens.

The fuck? we mutter.

But, really now—should we be surprised? We've witnessed the same changes—the bulldozing, the condos under construction, the advent of expensive chains whose net effect makes neighborhoods feel homogenous and impersonal, scrubbed of character and history, thus interchangeable with any other city populated by sky-scrapers and McDonald's. We've noted in these *up-and-coming!* neighborhoods, the inevitable accompanying influxes of whiteness also occurring in Bed-Stuy, Bush-wick, Harlem. We've heard stories from old-timers about what the Lower East Side and the Village used to be.

We learned about this particular photography ex-hibit from friends we went to art school with (our grad degrees boast RISD, UCLA, the Art Institute of Chi-cago, though never Pratt), and we've read reviews in *The New York Times* and *The New Yorker,* where critics at both publications deemed the exhibit *sensitive* and *life-altering* and *a deep portrayal of people of colors' struggles against* . . . blahblahblah. Because the exhibit is located in our old borough—albeit a neighborhood we never explored as girls on account of it being on the opposite end of the dregs of Queens—we decided to venture to see it.

When we enter the exhibit, we glance around, and immediately hate it.

Find that exhibit's premise and, by extension, the artwork, reeks of a posture so self-important and self-righteous, so *progressive,* that we must laugh in order not to snatch the photos from the wall and rip them to shreds. We leave.

On impulse, we ride the 7 to another part of Queens, five stops east of this neighborhood with its *breathtak-*

ing views of the Manhattan skyline! as advertised by real estate brokers—not to mention the $3,000 monthly rents in luxury apartment buildings, which is the price for this view.

When we arrive at our destination, we exit the station onto the old Boulevard of Death.

Trucks inch through traffic, and a call to prayer from a local mosque sounds, أَشْهَدُ أَنْ لَا إِلَهَ إِلَّا اللهُ،أَشْهَدُ أَنْ لَا إِلَهَ إِلَّا اللهُ! Horns blare around us. Smoke billows from beneath a manhole, an image so cliché it makes us roll our eyes and laugh at the same time. In this neighborhood, we crave momos, pork sisig, and beef empanadas, where just the scent flowing from the food trucks nearby causes us to salivate before we even sink our teeth into the flaky dough.

We didn't realize we'd been starving all along.

On our way to local restaurants—Sawasdee, La Tierra, Coco Malaysian, Tandoor N Talk, Nanay's—we pass a fabric store where bindis adorn the foreheads of otherwise featureless mannequins posing in store windows. We pass ads for immigration attorneys whose services include love and green card marriages, promises of EXPERIENCED ATTORNEYS WHO MAKE YOUR AMERICAN DREAM COME TRUE. We glance at businesses offering to ship items (outgrown winter coats, frying pans, chocolate bars to melt in mouths that have never been to dentists) to loved ones continents away. *Could you just send money next time?* some of our rela-

tives, exasperated, will ask after they open our families'
eclectic packages. Around us, music pours from cars,
causes us to stop. Listen.

Como la flor
Con tanto amor!
sings Selena, radiant.

And from an immaculate BMW, Shah Rukh Khan's
voice undulates:

तुम पास आये यूँ मुस्कराये...

as we recall watching *Kuch Kuch Hota Hai*
surrounded by our cousins.

Love songs, always. This time around, however, we
find that we aren't repelled by the noise, the chaos, in
the way we once were. The dregs of Queens, this place
we so desperately dreamt of leaving.

But who would've thought we'd long to return?

[+]

HOLY SHIT. IT'S FUCKING HAPPENING. WE GAZE, STUPEFIED, at the plastic sticks. First feeling: an exhilarating, wild, we-might-throw-up-we're-terrified-and-excited-like-we're-bungee-jumping-off-the-Brooklyn-Bridge-or-scuba-diving-for-the-first-time-God-we-hope-to-God-we-don't-fuck-it-up—first feeling for those of us who have done extensive ovary calculus, calendars and phone apps in hand. We've grabbed our partners, said, It's a full moon, and I'm fertile, let's go! and rushed into our beds. Some of us, however, blink once at the sticks. Blink twice, hard. Don't *tell* me this is for real. We walk calmly to the Rite Aid, CVS at the corner. Purchase Plan B for But I'm not ready. Plan B for But I fucked up. Take the pill. Gulp! Feel it scratch down our throats. Tell ourselves to not be so stupid next time, so *fucking* careless, though some of us will continue to make this same mistake. (*Loose American women!*) Others of us don't take the pill. Instead, we allow three days to elapse. One month, two, four. Say, Sayonara Plan B, Plan Bye-bye forever. Fine. Accidents we will keep.

We crave Cocoa Puffs in our ice cream, Spam fried on both sides, fruit salad made from canned ingredients with chewy, gelatinous textures, Arizona ninety-nine-cent cans of iced tea, mangoes not yet ripe, and Bud Light, which we can't drink, but it's okay—we just want to feel the aluminum can, cold, in our fists. Our bodies expand, as if the creatures growing inside us were galaxies. We lie, nauseous, on couches with these galaxy-babies, and stop, frightened, outside bodegas where toddlers ride mechanical ponies playing tinny music. *The wheels on the bus go—*

Only the most foolish of us feel ready.

Weeks pass. A black-hole feeling we pretend doesn't exist. A feeling we can't shake, which grows in our chests. We walk to the park where an ice cream truck blares its cheerful song. Where bikes whir and we hear the voices of families picnicking. Everything too, too bright. We press our bodies against the rails by the pier, where waves churn and crash on rocks. The odor of seaweed and New Jersey trash settles on our tongues. We stand, hands atop our not-yet-rounded bellies. Cargo ships enormous as space stations inch by. They're going somewhere, we think. While we remain rooted to the ground. Heat prickles our scalps, courses sluggishly through our throats, and morphs into a pain in our abdomens that forces us to sit down. We place our hands to our stomachs: six weeks. Think: too late?

(Wake up, emptied, on the doctor's table. At home, we pack away cans of paint, purchased but never opened, a crib half-assembled. *How could you do this?* our partners shout on the phone, on sidewalks, in bedrooms, where we cannot look at them. *You're a* FUCKING *psychopath*, they say. They throw their clothes into bags, leave for two weeks. Leave forever. They tell us to get out, to get the fuck out, and we do. We knock on our parents' doors in Queens. Or we don't. Stay when they shout, *This was supposed to be our—* Baby, we say. Calm down. Our lovers, who are no longer our lovers, we can see it in their eyes when they lie in bed that night, sleepless and silent. Strangers who do not utter a single word for an entire week. Except to say, *Well.* Except to say, *I never wanted it anyway, I never, never did* [but we know these are just words]. Except to say, *Are you happy now?*)

LITTLE FLAMES

MOMMY, CAN WE SWITCH EYES? OUR DAUGHTERS ASK. They are three, five, seven-and-a-half years old. We, in turn, are twenty-one, twenty-five, twenty-eight, thirty-two, thirty-seven, forty-three, forty-nine, though we feel we are one hundred, twelve, sixteen and a day all at once. *Mommy, I want to wear your skin!* Darling, we croon. First of all, that's creepy. And, second, why? You're already beautiful. We pinch their noses, help them brush their teeth, adhere temporary tattoos the shape of seahorses onto chubby arms, drag them away from the bodega's mechanical ponies, read books concerning mal-nourished caterpillars, ride the South Brooklyn–bound ferry and make up stories about what lies in the ocean beneath us. Once upon a time there was a monster with eyes that covered his entire body. He walked all over the earth, searching for another who looked just like him.

But when he couldn't find a creature with eyes from its head to its toes, he began to weep. His tears filled all the earth, the valleys and hollows where craters had once been. His tears flooded the whole world—*He was that sad?* our daughters ask. Yes, we say. And that's why we have oceans today. (Our daughters, who are now thirteen, fifteen, seventeen, remark, *That was a terrible story, Mom. So depressing!*) Our daughters whose complexions are the color of brick illuminated by sun, color of porcelain, color of a sunflower's dark center. Color of I-didn't-even-know-I-had-those-genes. Our daughters, our not-reflections. Who scrunch up their noses when they laugh, like we do, who fall asleep with their eyes half-open, like we do, until we kiss them shut. Who we believe, in our weakest moments, must be tamed as we had been tamed. Brush your hair, put on a dress, obey. Until we step back from their sleeping bodies.

What's this? Alarmed, we peer closer.

Discover a tiny flame hovering in the center of their chests. We cup our hands over its warmth. We jump back when it flares past our fingertips.

Our daughters, our daughters. Have our grandmother's wide-as-the-desert cheekbones, our father's thick, expressive eyebrows, or genes that don't belong to us at all, not in the least, but we don't give two shits—we know we were made for each other. Our daughters, who love puzzles and taking objects apart and reassembling them, who sketch outfits, entire cities, our galaxy and those beyond, as they imagine them, who wear nothing but the color forest green and sandals with socks for an entire year (we beg them not to, but they pay us no mind), who love walking through freshly fallen snow with us and sometimes with their grandmothers, and Sicilian pizza, whose Cheetos-colored oil we must wipe from their chins. Who decide they want to sing opera, too, when they stumble on us belting arias in the kitchen one day while we wash the dishes.

Our daughters, who ask us to tell them the story of our lives.

But what can we say about being a woman of color in this world?

Well, we begin, hesitantly. What is it you want to know?

Tell us about where you grew up, they say. *Tell us about Grandma and Grandpa. Who were your best friends? Who did you love most?*

We open our mouths, but no words come out. Not a proper sentence, save for a croak.

Instead, images flash through our minds: the dregs of Queens, our old block where the lone tree is now gone, the sidewalk smoothed over. Roots hidden, yet biding time to burst forth once again.

Do they know that everything that's part of us is also part of them?

To our children who have not yet been to our hometown, we promise: One day, we'll take you there.

Our daughters, our daughters, who don't yet know this world, but are filled with a spirit that cannot be tamed. They are three, four, five, seven-and-a-half years old. Who possess the power to snap us in two. Our brown girls. Strong enough for life itself. Or so we hope. We hope, and that is all we can do.

PART EIGHT

BROWN GIRLS ASCEND BEYOND THE FINAL FRONTIER & ALL I GOT WAS THIS LOUSY T-SHIRT

WE DIE.

And not in any metaphorical sense—not in the orgasmic ohmygosh-that-feels-so-good-you're-killing-me! sense, nor in the dead-to-self-alive-in-Christ-hallelujah! sense, nor the I-won't-acknowledge-your-existence-you're-dead-to-me! sense. But in the literal sense.

We die, and nobody likes to picture death.

Snapshot of Death #354—a mysterious, hitherto unknown virus

(—A *novel* virus.

—Wait, like a book?

—No, idiot! . . . Well, I suppose there *is* an overlap: "Novel," like, "new.")

breaks out in a country some of our parents had left behind. A place we'd traveled to as adults. Eventually, the virus—accompanied by an equally poisonous anti-Asian sentiment—reaches our own bright, shining, star-spangled shores, the Land of the Free (A-a-a-nd! The! Home! OF THE! BR—) *You do not have control,* the virus, now a worldwide pandemic, announces, if demon germs could speak.

In our neighborhoods, we join others and hoard hand sanitizer, cans of beans, pasta, rolls of toilet paper to wipe our asses, items to keep our precious bodies alive. Everyone's panic and fear and uncertainty all translate to: I DON'T WANT TO DIE I DON'T WANT TO DIE. Meanwhile, our mothers care for the sick and dying in city hospitals, now overflowing, having been virtually abandoned by the federal government (the president's busy golfing, and the virus is overblown, he claims).

Our mothers' simple recitation of their days to us, while we listen, our cell phones pressed to our ears until it hurts, awaken in us a respect and admiration so fierce, we realize we have never fully comprehended, nor understood, their line of work before.

In the U.S., disproportionate amounts of brown people are infected and killed. And yes, some of us joined them, too.

(March 2021: one year after New York's first lockdown. Projected U.S. death toll: 500,000 people.)

But whatever, that's not the point.

We die.

We could list all the additional ways we meet our ends over the years: accidental and random (caught in riptides, hit-and-runs, beneath ACs that fall on us— that shit's more common than you realize), purposeful and swift (we slit our wrists, we jump off bridges), purposeful and slow (bottles of booze, a pack of cigarettes each day), natural and boring (of old age surrounded by our loving families). We die from ailments lurking in our DNA and cells (heart attacks, cancers, aneurysms). We die purposely at the hands of another (our lives are cruelly taken from us, and we will haunt our killers on Earth and for eternity). Oh, there are so many ways we die, impossible and futile to list them all. So be content with this simple statement: We die, we die, we die.

Our old friend arrives in the dead of night, unannounced. Our roving eyeballs twitch back and forth behind our eyelids, thin as a butterfly's wings. It doesn't matter if our sheets boast a thread count of seven hundred, Egyptian cotton swaddling us from our waking worlds of global management, tech, academia. Or if we'd purchased our comforters for $29.99 (a steal!) at Kmart after we finished our paper-pushing, waitressing, nannying gigs for the day. Bulky bags in hand, we schlepped onto crowded subways headed home, where empty fridges awaited us. It doesn't matter if, lying in our beds, we now sleep beside strangers we met last night—we liked the way they looked at us—or if we slumber beside people we've known since we were eighteen, ones we'd woken beside ten, twenty, thirty years later to the realization that we had, in fact, fallen in love with them.

Well, shit, we mutter, then go back to sleep.

She arrives as we slumber, exhausted, children's books askew in our laps, our daughters burrowed beside us. Goodnight moon, we'd read, goodnight chair, goodnight red balloon.

She arrives as we slumber, sprawled across king-sized beds with silk eye masks shrouding our peepers— alone—just the way we like it.

The circumstances of our rest, the who what when where, don't matter: She meets us in our dreams. A state in which we are both alive and dead.

In dreams, we have been transported to weathered handball courts on middle school playgrounds that border a beach in the deepest dregs of Queens. A place where seagulls screech above chain-link fences and the funky scent of the Atlantic saturates the air. Our classmates' rowdy shouts ring around us. When we glance down at our bodies, we discover that we now inhabit our twelve-year-old selves: frizzy hair, one shoelace untied, a rash on our necks. Our laughter is bright and cruel.

When we catch sight of her dressed in her cotton gym uniform, we call her name.

Trish! we say.

Standing before us, not yet buried, dead, and gone—Trish looks as she did when we first met her: side-swept ponytail and that curious look.

Watch out, motherfuckers.

It's always been there, we realize.

We haven't laid eyes on her in decades. We thought we'd forgotten her face.

But minds don't forget, only file away.

Look how far you've come! Trish embraces us. *You're a nurse, a teacher, an artist. A wife, a mother. A grown-ass woman. All the things I never got to be.*

A curious sensation trickles over us. Guilt, then fear.

But who are you now? she says.

Trish takes our hand. She's morphed into a young woman. The beads on her black dress glimmer in the sunlight.

Why don't you visit me anymore? she asks.

Wake up! Our alarms sound—*ring ring ring!*—and herald the start of another day. Tears stream from our unopened eyes.

Her face was *exactly* how I remembered, we tell our partners, our cats, our roommates who stir their burnt coffees in shared kitchens. Or we tell nobody at all. Some of us, though, because we cannot shake her from our minds, text one another.

I know we haven't spoken in a while, we write, *but I had the craziest dream.*

Some of us do not wake up.

In the afterlife, we exist in a place that resembles outer space: its breadth and expanse, its frigid cold and bursts of light. We become exploding stars. We decompose. From our deteriorated bodies sprout our favorite plants: devil's ivy, fragrant magnolia trees, and blossoms whose names we never learned. In the afterlife, we exist on clouds. Not clouds that form in the atmosphere and blanket the earth—no, we exist on digital clouds. See: uploaded images of our smiling faces, every item we'd ever ordered, every random question we'd posed to that All-Knowing Being: our search engines. We exist in strange places that resemble the heavens described in sacred texts, our parents' Bibles and Korans and sutras. Places where, when we cut our hands, we barely bleed. When we meet the Creator, we feel like specks of dust. When we blink, She is gone, and we are surrounded, once again, by darkness. We discover that we are now a pool of water within a cave, black and unknowingly deep, the translucent onion skins that cling to our grown daughters' and our granddaughters' palms. We are the vertebrae of our grandparents' curved spines, their hands dusting soil from tomatoes growing in places most unlikely. We are the gnarled tree on the block. The one we'd biked past as children. Above our heads, the airplanes in the dregs of Queens roar. They are taking off or landing. We do not know which.

We die, we die, we die.

But take heart: We also live on.

We are shocked when Death greets us. Death is a shiver, a chill, a hand that reaches into our guts and squeezes tight. A few of us, understandably, cling on to life. If only I had, I wish I had—we do not win. Death arrives on a flaming chariot, mid-stroke while swimming in the Atlantic, she arrives in the dead of night, in a dream. Death sounds like a wind chime and a croak and the faintest whistling noise. She smells like the inside of sweaty sneakers and Chanel No. 5, and tastes like water purified by gravel in the Loire, cold and surprisingly, unsettlingly, bland. She tastes like shit. She tastes like the best thing we've ever tasted—swear on my mother's grave. *Shut up, already!* says Death, in the incarnation of our old friend. Trish takes our hand in hers. Fine, we say. We're ready. Let's go.

ACKNOWLEDGMENTS

I am grateful to the many people who have given this debut life.

Thank you, Jin Auh, for your guidance, forthrightness, and for being a fierce advocate. Thank you, Elizabeth Pratt, for being essential—I am indebted to both of you for your belief in my work, which has changed everything.

Huge thanks to Sarah Watling, Charles Buchan, Sarah Chalfant, and The Wylie Agency.

Thank you, Marie Pantojan. Your insightful questions and kindness helped me delve deeper into this story. Thank you for nurturing a version of this book that was greater than what I could have achieved on my own.

Thank you, Robin Desser and Andy Ward, for taking a chance on me. Thank you, Anna Kochman, June Park, and the art department for designing not only a gorgeous cover, but one that captures this book perfectly. Thank you, Avideh Bashirrad, Jennifer Rodriguez, Jo Ann Metsch, Kathleen Baldonado Reed, Deborah Bader, Edith Baltazar, and the entire Random House team— from production, permissions, marketing, publicity, sales, and beyond—for your hard work and dedication.

Thank you to my publishers abroad, who decided this story set in Queens was worth sharing with readers internationally: 4th Estate Books in the United Kingdom, Luchterhand in Germany, and Les Escales in France (so far)—thank you to the teams working on my behalf. A special thanks to Kishani Widyaratna.

Many organizations provided support throughout the years. Thank you, Martha's Vineyard Institute for Creative Writing and Sequoia Nagamatsu, for awarding an excerpt of *Brown Girls* the Voices of Color Fiction Fellowship. Thank you to the Edward F. Albee Foundation and Kimmel Harding Nelson Center for the Arts, which were peaceful settings for writing residencies. At the Sewanee Writers' Conference and the Bread Loaf Writers' Conference, I met wonderful, talented people and made lifelong friends. Huge thanks to the *Kenyon Review* for publishing an excerpt of *Brown Girls,* and to Mia Alvar, one of my favorite authors, for selecting my piece as winner of the Short Fiction Contest.

I am grateful to Nancy Drescher at The Family

Annex, Edit L. at Jadis, and my colleagues here, for supporting my work.

My deepest gratitude to my teachers, especially Elissa Schappell and Paul Beatty. Elissa, your classes changed my life and gave me the courage and freedom I needed to begin this project. Paul, you set high standards and pushed me to finish what I started. Thank you both for your generosity and ferocity. Thank you, Lara Vapnyar, Deborah Eisenberg, and Karan Mahajan for being incredible teachers. Thank you to Columbia University's MFA Writing Program, and to my workshopmates who shaped this project immensely.

Grace Schulman and Ely Shipley, thank you for those first lessons in poetry at CUNY Baruch College, which have always stayed with me.

Thank you, Shoshana Akabas, Karishma Jobanputra, Kaylen Baker, Morgan Thomas, and Krystel Gumpeng for reading early drafts with utmost care, patience, and intelligence. Thank you, Keira Graham, Christine Sicwaten, Naomi Brouard, and Blanche Palasi for allowing me to interview you, all those years ago. Thank you, Aileen Gumpeng, Justin Cuyan, 'Pemi Aguda, Josha, Jay, Nathan, and the many friends not listed here.

A huge thanks to the Andreades and Grisham clans for great conversations, as well as your love and unwavering encouragement over the years.

Several authors, including Crystal Hana Kim, generously shared their wisdom and time; to them, I'm grateful.

Much love and thanks to my family in Queens and Long Island—my aunties, uncles, cousins, grandparents. Your lives and journeys never cease to amaze me, fill me with pride, and inspire me. Thank you also to my loved ones in the Philippines.

Thank you, Jamison Galt, and my community at RCH.

To the many artists, especially the people of color, women, immigrants, and any combination of the above, who've come before me—thank you. Your work changed my life, and showed me it was possible, even necessary, to pursue art. Thank you for paving a path for me and others.

I am indebted to my parents, Dario and Catherine Palasi. Thank you, Dad, for modeling what it looks like to love and welcome all kinds of people. Thank you for always being present, and for taking us to the public libraries and bookstores week after week. Thank you, Mom, for demonstrating hard work, drive, and humbleness. Thank you both for sacrificing a great deal to give us a life full of opportunities, and for teaching me, in your own ways, to dream big and, more important, to work my butt off to reach these dreams. Thank you, Daryl and Blanche for your humor and warmth, and to Victoria Taclubao, one of the strongest people I know.

Thank you, above all, Thaddaeus Andreades. For

your faith in me and my work, and for telling me to keep going whenever I felt like giving up. Your kindness, creativity, delicious meals, and all the ways you love and care for us are a gift. I am so grateful to share a life with you.

Thank you, readers.

Thank you, God.